All About France

Peter Houldsworth

HODDER AND STOUGHTON

LONDON SYDNEY AUCKLAND TORONTO

Contents

Preface

All About France is intended to be used in a variety of ways and at various levels, both in schools and further or adult education colleges, or as a book of background information for the general public. The material contained in it has been presented in a straightforward manner, and yet in sufficient depth to satisfy a range of needs.

For school purposes it is assumed that the book will be used as follows:

1. As a down-to-earth classroom textbook (in conjunction with *Find Out About France*), suitable for the 13–16 year-old classes. I have deliberately avoided introducing the 'story' element commonly contained in books on this subject in order to produce a book which is capable of being *used* in the classroom, rather than a source of passive reading. In order to achieve this I have tried to include all the essential information required by pupils at this level, so as to avoid the all-too-frequent dependence on the *largesse* of the French Embassy! I have also assumed that the majority of teachers find it more convenient (as well as less costly) to have this information in a single book rather than scattered in a number of separate booklets and pamphlets, etc.

In order to make the book suitable for the working classroom situation, I have tried to provide a realistic framework for pupils' work and activities. *Find Out About France* contains a series of questions, exercises, projects etc. These have been roughly graded into straightforward factual questions, to which the answers can be found in this book, and topics to explore at slightly greater depth. *Find Out About France* has been produced separately in order to allow for greater flexibility in the use of *All About France*. In addition, pupils working under test conditions will be able to use *Find Out About France*

2. *All About France* may also be used on its own as a source of background information in Sixth Forms and Further and Adult Education Colleges, where there is usually a considerable interest in life in France, which cannot always be catered for in the time available.

3. It is hoped that *All About France* will also be of interest to the general public who wish to know more about life in France than is contained in guide books.

In conclusion I should like to express my gratitude to Mr Peter Downes (Headmaster, Henry Box School, Witney), as Editor, and to Mr P. D. Morris (Head of Modern Languages, Allerton Grange High School, Leeds), who acted as consultant, both of whom have given valued help and advice.

P.B.H.

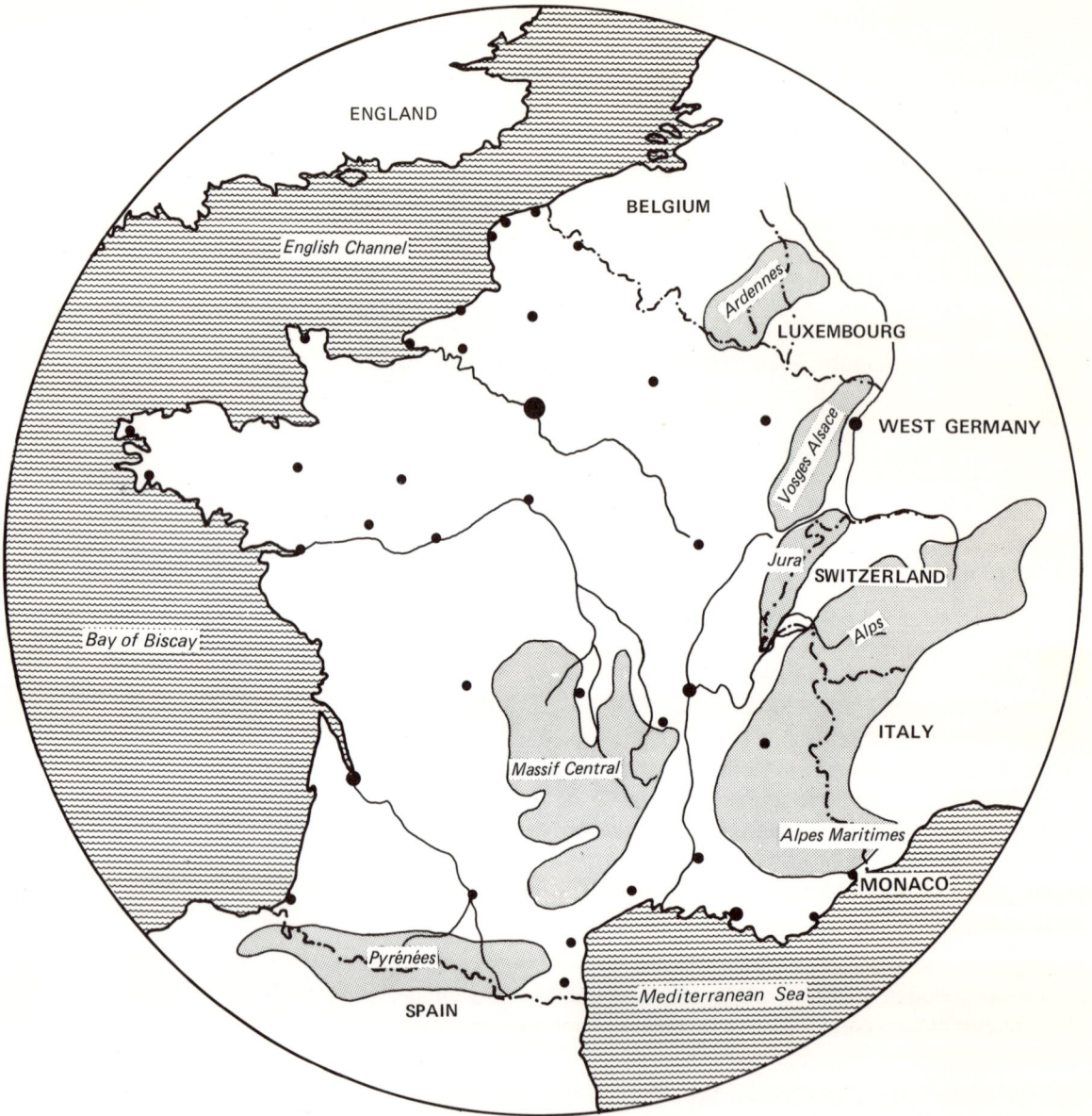

ENGLAND

English Channel

BELGIUM

Ardennes

LUXEMBOURG

WEST GERMANY

Vosges Alsace

Jura

SWITZERLAND

Alps

Bay of Biscay

ITALY

Massif Central

Alpes Maritimes

MONACO

Pyrénées

SPAIN

Mediterranean Sea

● Important towns (names are given in maps on pages 5 and 40)

France's natural frontiers

SECTION A: THE COUNTRY AND ITS PEOPLE

The country

France's frontiers and neighbours

As well as being Britain's nearest neighbour (little more than 30 kilometres away, at the nearest point), France is also the country through which many people have to travel if they are going by road or rail to other countries in Europe, whether on business or on holiday.

Neighbouring countries Look at the map on p. iv and you will see that the countries which border on France are Belgium, Luxembourg, Germany, Switzerland, Italy, Monaco and Spain. In several of these countries the French language is also spoken — in Belgium, Luxembourg, Switzerland and Monaco (although French is not the native language of all the inhabitants of all of these countries). Much of continental radio broadcasting is dominated by French, through stations such as Luxembourg, Europe No. 1, Monte Carlo, and Andorra. You can tune in on the average transistor radio to most of these stations, which broadcast mainly 'pop' music programmes.

Importance of its position The fact that France is surrounded by so many countries gives it a vital position in Western Europe, not only geographically, but also from an economic and political point of view. This has been reflected in the major role that France has taken in the development of the Common Market.

Mountains

The **Massif Central** includes the Auvergne and the Cévennes, and is a huge, thinly populated plateau, a large part of which covers southern and central France. (Its highest point is the **Plomb du Cantal**, 1886 m.) Down the Rhône valley blows the strong, cold wind called the *Mistral*, after which was named the record-breaking train, running from Paris to Marseilles.

The **Alps**, to the south-east, acting as a natural frontier to Italy and Switzerland, are the highest mountains in France, and include the highest peak in Europe: Mont Blanc (4807 m). This is a range of spectacular soaring mountains, where cultivation is possible only in the valleys. The snow which covers them all winter provides for one of the main activities of the area, which is winter sports.

The **Alpes Maritimes**, the Maritime Alps (which reach a height of 1912 m at Mont Ventoux) are an extension of the Alps, and as the

1

The rugged peaks of the Mont Blanc range (Photo Löis Jahan, DF)

name suggests, go down towards the sea. In fact they extend along the Mediterranean coast just inland, acting as a massive natural barrier or shelter to the coast. Their presence has had two enormous benefits for the narrow but luxuriant coastal strip of the Côte d'Azur (Riviera):

they shelter it from the winds blowing down from the Massif Central, which would otherwise have made the Riviera much colder and wetter;

they provide water from the snow and rain which fall on the mountains, and this has meant that the Riviera has had the perfect combination of hot sun and plentiful water that has created its 'Garden of Eden' character.

The **Pyrenees** to the south-west (rising to a height of 2877 m at the **Point du Midi de Bygorre**), form part of a natural frontier separating France from Spain. They are so steep that people can cross them only by using a series of passes. In the west of this area is the home of the Basques, a very independent people with their own language, who live partly in Spain and partly in France.

The **Jura** mountain range which is really an extension of the Alps, although not as high (1723 m at its highest point), forms part of the natural frontier with Switzerland, and is characterised by a series of parallel valleys, which cross the forests and plains.

To the east the **Vosges**, through which the Rhine has cut a deep gorge, form part of the eastern frontier with Germany, and rise to 1366 m at **Hohneck**. This is an area of rolling hills, lakes and pine forests.

*A petrol tanker entering the Port of Marseilles (*Port autonome de Marseille*)*

Rivers and ports

The **Seine** (776 km long) flows through **Paris** (which is France's largest river port) and the Paris Basin. It goes on through **Rouen** (France's third-ranking river port) to the port of **Le Havre**. In the amount of trade it handles, Le Havre is second only to **Marseilles** (spelt 'Marseille', with no 's' in French). The Seine is the busiest waterway in France, and every day you can see the big continental barges, laden with cargo, chugging their way through the centre of Paris.

The **Loire** (1010 km long), France's longest river, flows through some of France's most famous wine-growing areas, as well as through the historic towns of **Orleans** and **Tours**, to the Atlantic, and to the busy ports of **Nantes** and **Saint-Nazaire**. The valley of the Loire is one of the beauty spots of Europe, much visited by tourists.

The **Rhône** (864 km long) and its giant tributary the **Saône**, which joins it at **Lyons** (spelt 'Lyon' in French), flows into the Mediterranean at Marseilles, which is France's major port. The force of the Rhône has nowadays been harnessed to a great series of dams and hydro-electric power stations, on which the economy of a large part of southern France depends.

The **Garonne** (650 km long) flows, like the Loire, through extensive wine-growing areas, to the Atlantic and the port of **Bordeaux**, which is one of the great centres of the French wine trade. The upper reaches of the Garonne provide electric power for much of south-west France.

The **Rhine** (1320 km long) flows through other countries as well as France. It is not only Europe's busiest river, but it also acts as a natural frontier (180 km long) between France and Germany. **Strasbourg** is the port which handles most of the French traffic on the Rhine, and is the second busiest river port in France, as well as a source of electric power.

A convoy of river barges entering the port of Strasbourg (Photo Novestair – Port autonome de Strasbourg)

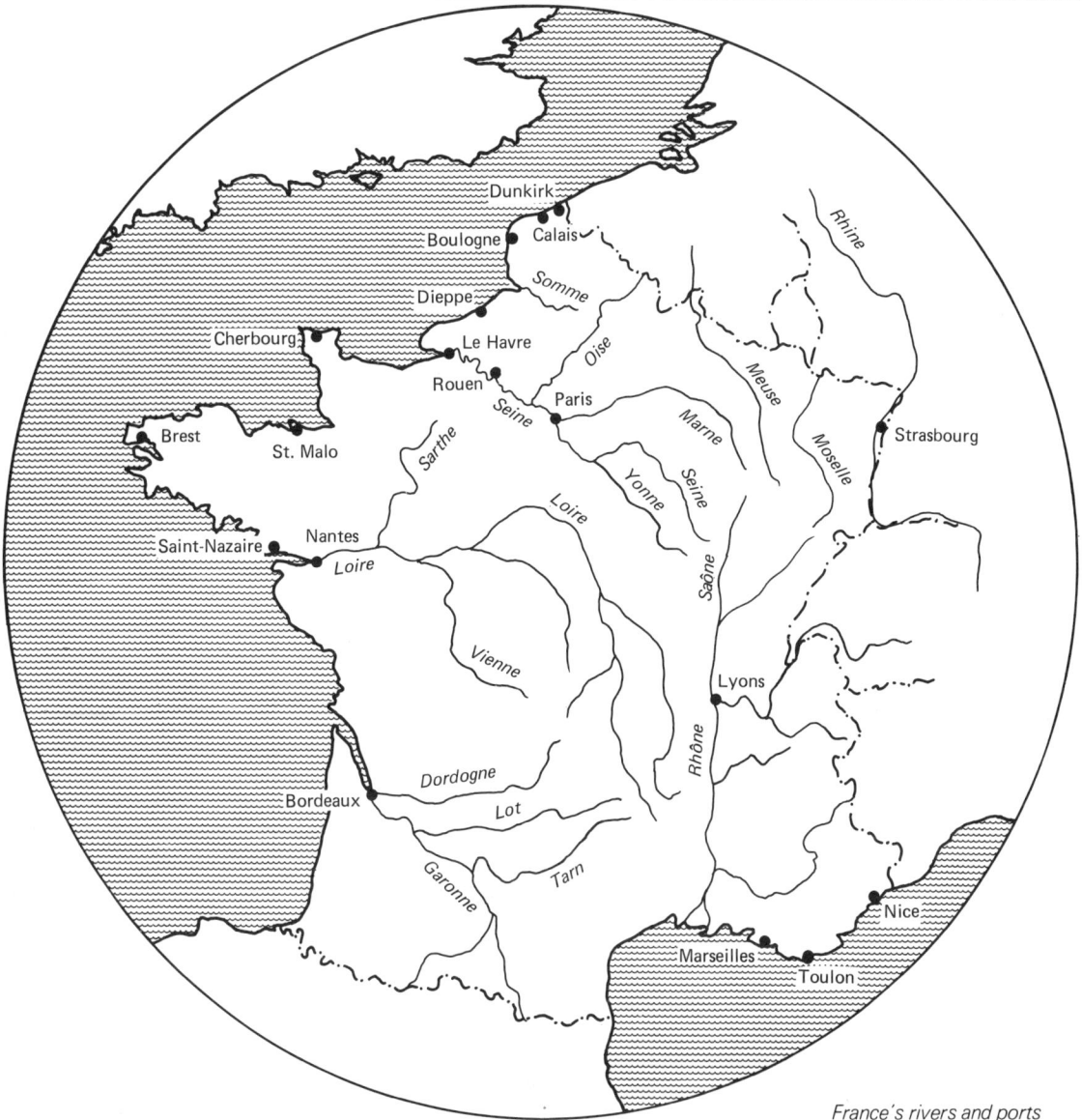

France's rivers and ports

Port	Millions of Tonnes	10 million tonnes
Marseilles	64.9	
Le Havre	49.2	
Paris	25.0	
Dunkirk	20.8	
Rouen	11.7	
Nantes/St. Nazaire	11.4	
Bordeaux	8.7	

Trade handled by France's main ports

The people of France

Variety

Many people who do not know France well are tempted to lump all French people together as though they were all the same. But they sometimes forget that the French are a mixture of people each with their own distinctive character, culture and traditions, and even their own language (e.g. Basque, Breton, Catalan, Alsatian, Corsican). You have only to visit some of the areas where these people live to realise when you talk to them just how much they consider themselves to be different from French people of other parts of France.

The terrace of a crowded café on the Champs-Elysées (Photo Camboroque – DF)

Size of population

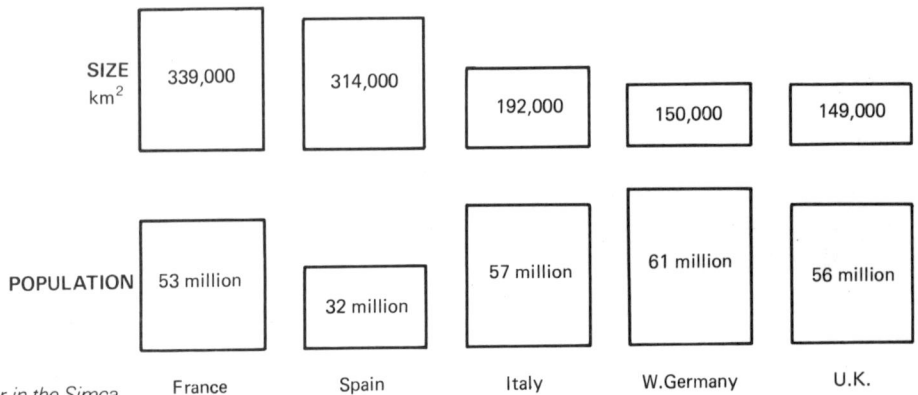

SIZE km²	339,000	314,000	192,000	150,000	149,000
POPULATION	53 million	32 million	57 million	61 million	56 million
	France	Spain	Italy	W.Germany	U.K.

Below, a foreign worker in the Simca factory near Paris (Photo Simca)

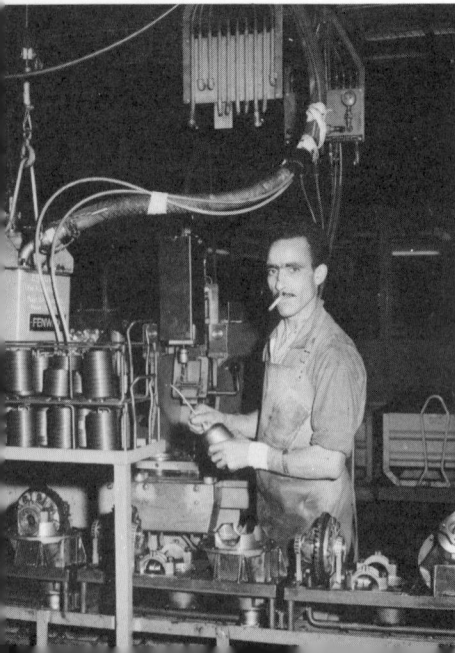

Look at the diagram above, showing the size of France and its population, compared with its most important neighbours, and you will see that:

Land. France has the largest land area of any country in Western Europe (in places it is as much as 1000 km across);

People. The population is less than that of several countries which are smaller in size, including Britain, West Germany and Italy. This is in spite of the fact that there are over two and a half million foreigners in France, most of whom are immigrant workers from North Africa, Spain and Portugal, as well as nearly a million people of French origin who returned from the former French colonies of Algeria and Morocco when these countries became independent.

These two factors explain why you have such a great sense of space when travelling through France, for there are large areas with very few inhabitants, and virtually no towns or even villages.

Compared to most other countries in Europe, France is an under-populated country, as we can see from this diagram, which shows the number of people per square kilometre.

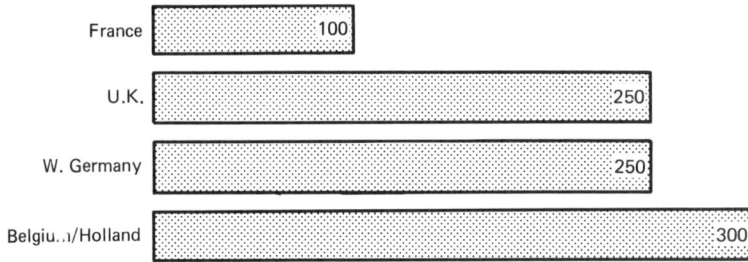

France	100
U.K.	250
W. Germany	250
Belgiu..ı/Holland	300

Centres of population

France has remained a less industrialised country than Britain or West Germany, and industrial development has been mainly concentrated in a few towns only, as you can see from the diagram below.

French industry in full production: the assembly line at the Renault car factory (Photo Renault)

These figures relate to the towns themselves and do not include the outer suburbs. Nevertheless, it is striking that Paris is the only town in France with over a million people; apart from Paris only Marseilles has a population of over half a million; five other towns have a population of over a quarter of a million.

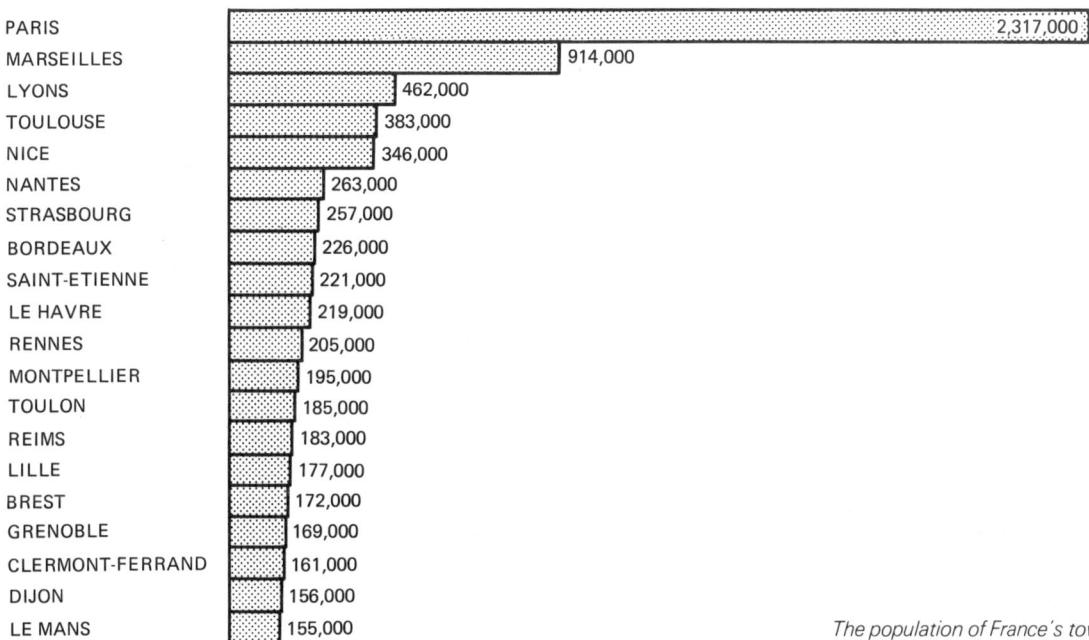

PARIS	2,317,000
MARSEILLES	914,000
LYONS	462,000
TOULOUSE	383,000
NICE	346,000
NANTES	263,000
STRASBOURG	257,000
BORDEAUX	226,000
SAINT-ETIENNE	221,000
LE HAVRE	219,000
RENNES	205,000
MONTPELLIER	195,000
TOULON	185,000
REIMS	183,000
LILLE	177,000
BREST	172,000
GRENOBLE	169,000
CLERMONT-FERRAND	161,000
DIJON	156,000
LE MANS	155,000

The population of France's towns

Work

Types of jobs in France

TYPES OF JOBS		NO. & PROPORTION OF PEOPLE EMPLOYED (IN THOUSANDS)			
		1968	1975		Percentage increase or decrease
		Number	Number	%	
	Manual Workers	7,706	8,207	32.2%	+ 0.9%
	Clerical Workers	2,996	3,841	17.6%	+ 3.6%
	Middle Management	2,006	2,765	12.7%	+ 4.7%
	Agriculture	3,048	2,006	9.2%	– 5.8%
	Self-employed	1,995	1,709	7.8%	– 1.9%
	Professional and Senior Management (incl. teachers)	995	1,459	6.8%	+ 5.6%
	Service jobs (incl. cleaners)	1,166	1,244	5.7%	+ 0.9%
	Others (e.g. artists, clergy)	526	524	2.4%	– 0.1%

The traditional methods of farming: an older farm worker gathering artichokes on a small farm in Finistère (Photo FAT – DF)

You will see from the diagram above that over recent years there has been a decrease mainly in agricultural workers and to some extent in the number of self-employed, but an increase in both clerical and managerial jobs. In other words people have been leaving the land to take up office jobs, although the largest number of people are still doing manual work.

Agriculture

Farming and agriculture have traditionally been one of the main sources of jobs and national income in France; and even today, although agriculture plays a lesser role in the country's economy, France is still capable of feeding the entire population from its own resources, and produces and exports more agricultural goods than any other country in the Common Market. This helps to explain why the French are particularly concerned about agriculture, compared to other countries in the Common Market, and why France has played a leading role in developing the controversial EEC Common Agricultural Policy.

You can see from the diagram on p. 9 that the most widely grown crops are cereals (especially wheat), with fodder or animal feeding crops and root crops as the other main produce.

TYPES OF CROP	AREA OF LAND IN HECTARES (1 Hectare - 2.47 acres)
Cereals	9,222
Cereal Seeds	164
Root Crops	1,533
Textile Crops	39
Oil seeds and Olive Oil	359
Various industrial crops	26
Medicinal & perfume crops	31
Vegetables	310
Fruit	9
Fodder crops	5,046
Other seeds for principal crops	72
Fallow land	384

The use of farm land

Although France produces a great deal of food for export, you can see from the diagram above that she has not enough meat, vegetables and oils, which have to be imported.

France shares first place with Italy as the world's largest producer of wine, which is produced more or less everywhere in France south of a line drawn between Brest and Strasbourg. The quality varies from region to region, with some such as Bordeaux, Burgundy and Champagne specialising in the high-quality and vintage wines; others such as Languedoc, Roussillon and Provence (i.e. the more southerly parts) producing mainly cheaper table wines.

France's agricultural imports / exports

The relative income from France's agricultural crops

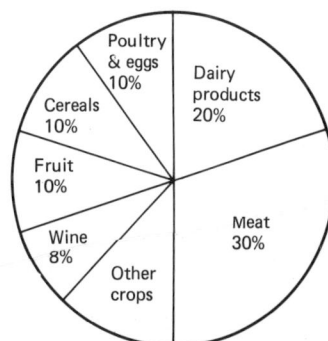

Agricultural jobs

Methods of farming in France have changed radically during the last twenty years, as farming has become increasingly mechanised. The result has been that fewer and fewer people have been needed, and every year an average of 150 000 farm workers have left the countryside to take jobs in the towns. In ten years the number of people working in agriculture has almost halved, and the number of farms has also been reduced by a third over a period of fifteen years, though this has often been in order to create larger farms of a more economic size. As in most other countries, modern methods and larger farms are now turning farming into an industry, and French farming will have been transformed almost within a generation out of the middle ages into the twenty-first century.

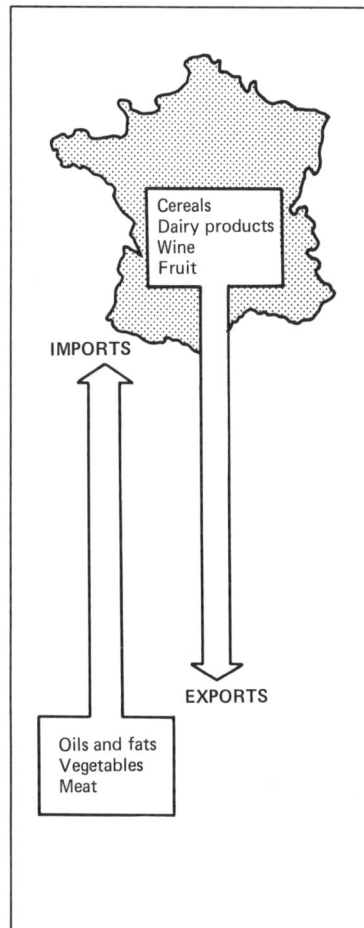

A nuclear power station at Chinon on the Loire: a part of France's huge nuclear programme designed to offset her lack of natural energy sources (Photo EDF – M. Brigaud)

The solar energy laboratory at Odeillo-Font-Romeu: one of the new forms of energy with which France is experimenting (Photo G. Ehrmann – Sodel, EDF)

Industry

The period since the war has seen the rebuilding and modernisation of French industry as well as the introduction of new industries, sometimes in addition to, but often replacing the older, traditional industries. France is now the fourth largest exporting country in the world. The first post-war plan concentrated on building up the basic industries of iron and steel, fuel and power, railways, cars and aeroplanes, chemicals and machinery.

Energy Fuel and power in particular are a continuing problem for France, which has little oil or coal, and only a limited amount of natural gas (at Lacq in the south-west). This explains why France has embarked on a large-scale programme of nuclear power stations, which will supply a quarter of France's energy by 1985, and on the exploitation of hydro-electric power from the rivers. She is also a leader in experimental forms of energy: tidal energy from the sea (e.g. the **Rance** tidal power station); and power from the sun (e.g. the solar power station at **Odeillo**, in the south).

Modernisation Under the impulse of the Common Market, industry and commerce have had to introduce modern machinery and techniques, and to reorganise into larger, more effective units in order to compete on a European and world-wide scale: examples of this are in the motor industry as well as many others.

Decentralisation Part of the problem facing the government in the long-term planning of French industry has been the same as in many other aspects of French life: too great a concentration of jobs and workers, particularly in the Paris region, but also to a lesser extent in the Rhône-Alps and northern industrial regions, which between them provide nearly half the industrial jobs of the whole country. The government has therefore tried to encourage the spread of industries into areas which have previously been largely agricultural.

SECTION B: DAILY LIFE IN FRANCE

The family

The family has always been a very important part of French life, and it is a tradition which has been encouraged by the Church. Even though not as many French people go to church as formerly, the tradition of the importance of the family has been maintained.

Marriage

When a couple marry in France, they usually go through two marriage ceremonies:

The **civil marriage** – conducted at the *mairie* or *hôtel de ville* (town hall) by either the mayor or his deputy, who wears the red, white and blue tricolour sash, which is his badge of office. This is the legal contract.

The **church marriage** – usually straight after the civil ceremony the couple go from the town hall to the church, where a religious service (or wedding mass) is held.

Children

French couples are encouraged by the state (through its system of family allowances) to have more than one child. This is because the population is considered to be too low in relation to the size of the country: the expansion of population was affected by the loss during the two World Wars of over one and a half million men, who would have been fathers of many children.

In addition to family allowances, mothers who have several children can win medals (*médailles de la famille française*).

A civil marriage (Photo P. J. Downes)

Baptism

Most French children are baptised in the Roman Catholic Church. This is the reason so many children have a double Christian name, such as Jean-Claude or Marie-Françoise: the Church requires one name to be the name of a saint, which is usually added at Confirmation.

Birthdays

French people appear to have two birthdays. In fact one is a Saint's day or *fête*; the birthday proper is the *anniversaire*.

French children tend to stay up later at night with their parents than English children and join more in family life, which still centres round meals, in spite of the increasing influence of television.

Parents

Although the father retains much of his traditional authority as the head of the family (*le chef de famille*), the mother remains very much at the centre of family life, in spite of the increasing number of mothers who return to work nowadays.

Divorce

Divorce is less common in France than in the Anglo-Saxon countries such as Britain and the USA, or in Russia. The number of divorces is actually decreasing in France: only eight per cent of marriages end in divorce.

Women's rights

Women now have equal rights with men, and are entitled by law (since 1946) to the same salary for the same job. Thirty-five per cent of the total working population are women, but in contrast to Britain and many other western countries, French women have only had the right to vote since 1944.

Women working on the assembly line in a factory making transistors at Aix-en-Provence (Photo Thompson – CSF – R. Videt)

Young people

The result of the government's policy of encouraging couples to have more children is that the population now contains more young people than it has done for many years.

Much more effort is made nowadays to cater for young people and their interests. Some radio programmes and even radio stations (such as Europe No. 1, on 1647 metres), are devoted to pop music, which is often British or American music with French words. A number of magazines are published which are specially for teenagers, e.g. *Salut les Copains*, which originally took its name from the title of a pop music programme on Europe No. 1, but is now a general magazine for teenagers. Catering particularly for teenage girls, *Mlle Age Tendre* contains articles on fashion, cinema, etc., as well as the usual letters from readers.

Although young people go to *discothèques*, many prefer to go to *surprise-parties* at friends' houses, where they will play records and dance. So young French people tend to stay among their own groups of friends rather more than in the case of Anglo-Saxon countries.

Young people spend many hours going to cafés, where they can drink and talk to their friends. Many become quite expert at making one drink last a long time, for the café is often the main social centre and meeting place for the young, as well as for the older generation.

More young people take up sports nowadays. This is because sport is now included in school timetables, and because the government has provided funds for more facilities, such as swimming-pools, athletics tracks, etc. Among the most popular sports for young people are football, rugby, volleyball and skiing in the winter, and athletics, swimming and tennis in the summer.

Young people using a modern gymnasium: an example of France's increasing provision of facilities for sport and recreation (Photo INSEP)

Education

Background

French schools belong to two categories: church schools, and those run by the state, which are the majority (80 per cent). Before 1968 the state system had been dominated by the prestigious *lycées* (or grammar schools), which had been set up by Napoleon and aimed at producing an élite of the most able students, who took their *baccalauréat* examination prior to going on to university. The rest went to junior secondary schools, and if they were good enough took various other examinations of a lower level.

Narrow curriculum Until 1968 education in France had followed the traditional lines which had not changed significantly since long before 1939. The secondary schools, and in particular the *lycées*, had followed a predominantly classical curriculum, under which pupils were expected to work hard, but given little opportunity to follow broader interests or to play much sport. Discipline had been strict and teachers had used largely old-fashioned 'chalk and talk' methods, which required pupils to memorise large parts of their work: few of the newer and more stimulating teaching aids and types of equipment had been introduced. Teachers tended to come and give their lessons and then depart without really getting to know their pupils

Young French children at break (Photo INRDP – Jean Suquet)

Events of May 1968

Although selection for secondary schools had been abolished in 1957, it was not until May 1968 that the dissatisfaction with the education system came to a head. In the so-called '*événements de mai*' (events of May) many thousands of university and *lycée* students, supported by many of their teachers, took part in a series of riots and demonstrations against the old system in France, complaining of poor conditions in the classroom and over-crowded classes which prevented students and teachers getting to know each other. Students had felt increasingly dissatisfied with the over-traditional nature of the subjects taught in school, as well as with the non-progressive and often unimaginative methods which were used to teach them. In short, it was felt that schools had got out of touch with the needs of modern society.

Reforms

As a result of this mounting and often violent expression of discontent, a series of measures was introduced with a view to reforming the education system along more modern and progressive lines.

One of the most important new measures removed much of the power from the *directeur* (head teacher) and put the running of each school in the hands of a more democratic school council (*conseil d'administration*), made up of representatives of teachers, parents, pupils and the Ministry of Education.

Within the schools, each class was to have its own council (*conseil de classe*), consisting of the head teacher, the school doctor and social welfare officer, careers adviser, teachers and representatives of parents and pupils. This council was concerned with results and progress, and general class problems, including discipline and careers advice.

During recent years education has become an increasing cause of concern and political debate, and this is reflected in the increasingly large proportion of France's total budget that has been devoted to it.

In fact more money is spent on education, in one form or another, than on any other single item, more even than on defence or health and social security.

Some interesting features of French schools

Most French children go to free state schools, which are all under central control from Paris.

There are also a number of private schools, mostly Catholic, run by priests and nuns.

Compulsory schooling is from the age of six until sixteen years of age.

The school year usually starts in the middle of September.

Summer holidays (*les grandes vacances*) are about ten weeks long: but Christmas and Easter holidays are short (only a few days).

Wednesday is usually a free day in French schools — but in many schools there are lessons on Saturday mornings. However the trend is increasingly towards an English type weekend, with no Saturday morning school.

In secondary schools, classes usually begin at 8 o'clock in the morning and go on until 5 o'clock in the afternoon, though they have a number of free periods.

In French schools, classes are usually numbered backwards from Class 11 to Class 1. The first year class in the lower secondary school is called the sixth form.

All French secondary schools have the same curriculum and examinations, determined by the Ministry of Education.

Many state secondary schools are partly boarding schools. Pupils who live in country areas or a long way from school often live as boarders (*internes*). Day pupils are called *externes*. Those who stay to lunch are called *demi-pensionnaires*.

AGE	CLASS	SCHOOL	EXAMINATIONS
15-18/19 yrs (*2nd cycle*)	Terminal	Upper Secondary School (*Lycée*)	*Baccalauréat* or Technician's diploma
	1^e		*C.A.P.* (Vocational Diploma)
	2^e		
11-15/16 yrs (*1st cycle*)	3^e	Lower Secondary School (*Collège*)	*B.E.P.C.* (School Leaving Certificate)
	4^e		
	5^e		
	6^e		
6-11 yrs (*elementary studies*)	7^e	Junior School (*Ecole Primaire*)	
	8^e		
	9^e		
	10^e		
	11^e		
2-6 yrs		Nursery School (*Ecole Maternelle*)	

The French school system

Age 2–6: nursery school (*école maternelle*)

Many children in France go to nursery schools: it is quite usual for them to start at the age of two, but they are not required by law to go to school until they are six.

Unlike the later stages of French schooling, the nursery school curriculum is not set by Paris, and includes different sorts of activities such as drawing, modelling, singing, stories, painting etc.

In addition to the state nursery schools, there are private nursery schools or kindergartens (*jardins d'enfants*), to which parents pay to send their children.

Age 6–11: primary school (*école primaire*)

At the age of six, all French children have to go to a primary school (*école primaire*), no matter whether they have been to a nursery school or not. These are usually mixed. Though there is no uniform, some children, particularly in country schools, wear a kind of grey overall or smock (*tablier*) over their ordinary clothes.

A primary school class in action (Photo INRDP – Jean Suquet)

For the first two years children are taught to read, write and count. From the third year they learn French (ten hours), arithmetic (five hours), history, geography, science, civics, art and music (six hours total); physical training and sport (six hours); and later there is some homework.

The children have no examination at the age of eleven, when they finish at the primary school and go on to the secondary school (*collège*).

Special classes

In many schools children are taken to the mountains for winter sports (*classes de neige*), to the sea-side (*classes de mer*), and to the country (*classes vertes*).

Centres de vacances For some years holiday centres known as *colonies de vacances* provided holiday breaks for children from poorer homes, but these have been replaced by holiday and leisure centres (*centres de vacances*) offering organised holidays which are available to children from every social background. By 1976 over 12 000 holiday centres had been established, providing holidays for 1·4 million children between four and eighteen years of age.

These centres try to provide for a range of activities, particularly outdoor activities such as walking, climbing, sailing, canoeing, building log huts, learning crafts, nature conservation schemes, etc. These activities offer the children the opportunity to widen their interests whilst enjoying themselves – a combination of fun and education.

A college d'enseignement secondaire (CES) – *pupils arriving for morning school (Photo INRDP – Pierre Allard)*

Age 11–15/16: lower secondary school (*collège*)

This is the first stage of secondary school and is called the *premier cycle* (first cycle).

The *collèges* are basically comprehensive, and for the first two years the children are in unstreamed classes, i.e. they are not split into different classes according to ability. This stage is called the *cycle d'orientation*, during which it is decided which sort of course each child will be best suited to.

During these first two years, all children take the same subjects, which are those they had studied at the primary school, plus one new subject (a foreign language, usually English). The subjects studied are: French, a foreign language, maths, economic and human sciences, manual skills, art, music and sport. These subjects are decided not by individual schools or head-teachers, but by the Ministry of Education in Paris.

During the last two or three years, students continue with the same basic subjects, but at the beginning of the third year they have a choice of additional subjects, according to whether they enter:

(a) *academic stream*: taking either a second modern language, *or* more science subjects *or* Latin and Greek. This is the *lycée stream*.

(b) *vocational stream*: taking classes, combined with periods in industry, to show them the different sorts of jobs and trades for which they can train.

Examinations

Before they leave the *collège* students can take a school leaving examination, called the *BEPC* (*Brevet d'Etudes du Premier Cycle*). Those who have not reached this stage by the time they are due to leave school can take a one-year apprentice training at a *CFA* (*Centre de Formation d'Apprentis*).

Upper secondary schools (*lycées*)

When students leave the *collège*, they can either take a job, do a year's apprentice training, or continue their schooling at a *lycée*. The *lycées* are the second cycle or stage of secondary schooling, and students usually go there at either fifteen or sixteen. How long they continue their studies depends on their choice, for there are two kinds of *lycée*:

1. *LEGT: Lycées d'Enseignement Général et Technologique*

Here they follow a three-year course leading to one of two kinds of examination:

(a) the *Baccalauréat* (*bachot* or *bac* in familiar speech)

or

(b) the *Brevet de Technicien* (*BT*).

These examinations allow them to go on to university or higher

A class at work in a lycée *(Photo INRDP – Jean Suquet)*

education.

2. *LEP: Lycées d'Enseignement Professionel*

   These schools offer a two-year vocational or professional course, leading to one of two other kinds of examination:

   (a) *BEP: Brevet d'Etudes Professionelles* (for supervisory types of jobs)

   or

   (b) *CAP: Certificat d'Aptitude Professionelle* (for skilled manual workers).

   Students often stay on at *lycées* after these examinations, even until the age of twenty or twenty-one. They may be preparing to take either a higher technical diploma, or the very difficult examinations for one of the *grandes écoles*, the great prestige colleges for state jobs. The classes in which they study are called *terminale*.

Higher education

Students who have passed the *baccalauréat* have a choice:

1. *Les Ecoles Normales*

   They can go to an *école normale* (teacher training college), to train to be an *instituteur* in a primary school or a teacher in a *collège*.

2. *Les UER (Unités d'Enseignement et de Recherche)*

   Any student who has passed the *baccalauréat* has an automatic right to a place in a university or *UER*. These are the new university institutions, which were set up after May 1968, when the thirteen old universities were reorganised and split up into 64 new universities (thirteen of which are in Paris). The old university faculties were set up as separate universities, called *UER*. At the same time new institutions of higher education called *IUTs* (*Instituts Universitaires de Technologie*) were set up to provide advanced technical and vocational training.

A lecture taking place in a university lecture theatre (Photo INRDP – Pierre Allard)

3. *Les Grandes Ecoles*

The *grandes écoles*, which have a great prestige in France, are special colleges which prepare their students, most of whom receive a salary while they are studying, for some of the top jobs in the various departments of the government service. Amongst the most famous of the *grandes écoles* are:

L'Ecole Polytechnique (founded by Napoleon) training technologists;

L'Ecole Normale Supérieure training high-level teachers;

L'Ecole Nationale d'Administration (known as *l'ENA*) (founded by General de Gaulle) training France's top civil servants.

L'Ecole des Sciences Politiques (*Sciences Po'*), France's leading School of Economics.

Leisure activities

French people have similar kinds of leisure activities to their counterparts in other countries, though the pattern is often different.

For the majority of French people, the most common leisure activity is to go to a restaurant or café for a meal or drinks with friends. More than in almost any other country, the leisure activities are centred round restaurants and cafés, which represent the real social centres of French life.

Interest in theatre and concerts is concentrated largely on Paris, which provides the most opportunities. In the past, there have been few theatres or concerts outside Paris, though efforts are being made to encourage more of such activities in the provinces.

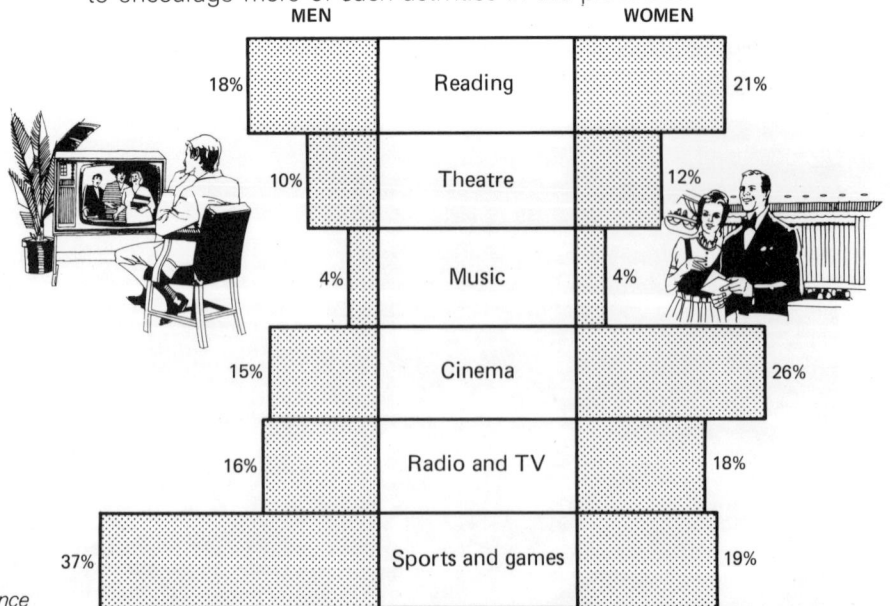

MEN		WOMEN
18%	Reading	21%
10%	Theatre	12%
4%	Music	4%
15%	Cinema	26%
16%	Radio and TV	18%
37%	Sports and games	19%

Favourite leisure activities in France

The media

Radio and television

French radio and television are run by the *Radio Télévision Française* (*RTF*) which has replaced the old *ORTF*. The latter was a single organisation controlling directly all French radio and television, but it has now been split up into a looser organisation, with each of the radio and television channels operating independently, under the general control of the *RTF*. The headquarters of the *RTF* is in the ultra-modern new building of the *Maison de la Radio*, though most television work is done in other buildings.

The *RTF* controls the three main channels and three television channels; even though they are state-run, they include commercials.

Radio channels

1. *France Inter*: news, variety and music.
2. *France Culture*: cultural and educational programmes.
3. *France Musique*: classical music.

Commercial radio

In addition to the state radio channels the following independent commercial stations broadcast largely pop music to France from neighbouring countries:

Radio Monte Carlo in Monaco
Radio Luxembourg
Radio Andorra
Europe No. 1 from Saar in Germany.

Guide to television programmes
(Photo P. J. Downes)

The impressive building of the Maison de la Radio (Radio France. Photo Roger Picard)

Television channels

There are three television channels, (*TF1*, *A2* and *FR3*) which, although state-run, include commercials. French people tend to spend less time watching television than people in some countries, largely because the evening meal in France not only takes longer, but plays a more important part in the life of the average French family. In addition to this French television programmes have not always been of a very high standard.

The press

It has been estimated that six out of every ten French people over the age of eighteen read at least one newspaper every day.

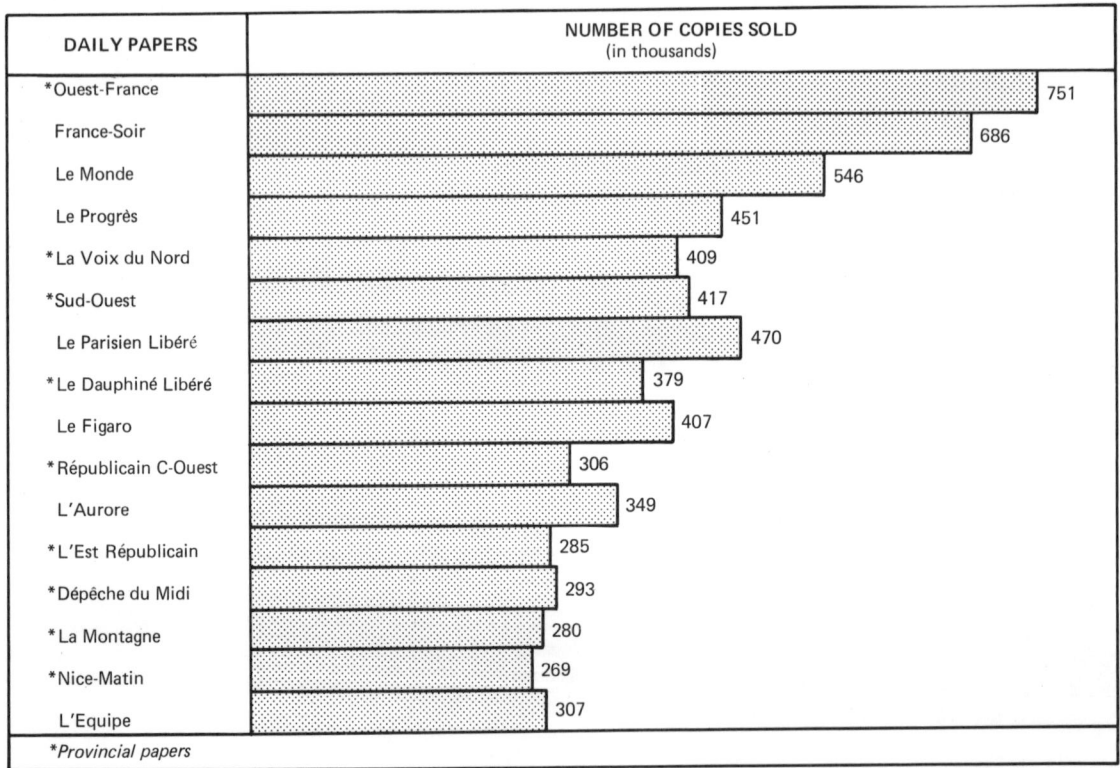

DAILY PAPERS	NUMBER OF COPIES SOLD (in thousands)
*Ouest-France	751
France-Soir	686
Le Monde	546
Le Progrès	451
*La Voix du Nord	409
*Sud-Ouest	417
Le Parisien Libéré	470
*Le Dauphiné Libéré	379
Le Figaro	407
*Républicain C-Ouest	306
L'Aurore	349
*L'Est Républicain	285
*Dépêche du Midi	293
*La Montagne	280
*Nice-Matin	269
L'Equipe	307
*Provincial papers	

The main French daily newspapers and their circulation figures

Strong provincial press Looking at the diagram above, one of the most striking things is the number and strength of the provincial papers, which have a much wider circulation than in most countries. A result of the strength of the provincial press in France is to weaken the national press: this is a feature which is unique among European countries (although it applies even more in the USA). The national press is gradually becoming more concentrated, and the number of national newspapers has decreased by more than half in the last twenty years.

Sport

Traditionally the French have never been very interested in sport. This was because sport was not encouraged in the schools, which had few facilities such as sports grounds, swimming pools or gymnasia, and where games and PE did not appear on the timetable.

Since the end of the last century, however, sport has become increasingly popular, particularly since the 1950s when the government has provided increasing support and money for sport. It was felt that more should be done to encourage sport, both to promote fitness and for reasons of national prestige. (It is no accident that the concern for national sporting prestige should coincide with the period when General de Gaulle was in power!)

An athletics training session (Photo INRDP – Pierre Allard)

New facilities The government has provided increasing amounts of money to the various sporting associations: eight times as much in 1968 as in 1958. Within a period of five years more swimming pools were built than in the previous forty years. Between 1957 and 1976, the number of sports stadia and sports grounds rose from approximately 9500 to 42 500, while that of gymnasia increased from 1500 to 11 500 and swimming pools from 500 to 2500.

Numbers of people registered for different sports

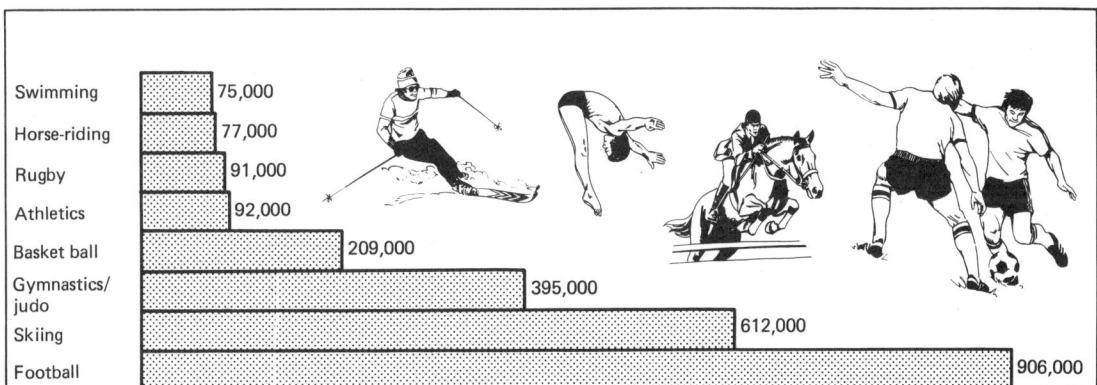

Sport	Number
Swimming	75,000
Horse-riding	77,000
Rugby	91,000
Athletics	92,000
Basket ball	209,000
Gymnastics/judo	395,000
Skiing	612,000
Football	906,000

Registration system People who want to take a serious interest in sport have to become registered (or *licencié*) with the sporting body or association responsible for the particular sport. But this does not mean that the only people who practice a sport are those with a *licence*. For example, over two million French people go skiing, but only about a quarter of that number (580 000) are actually registered. The number of people registered for sports is shown in the diagram on the previous page.

Cycling

It is interesting to see that cycling, which is one of the traditional French sporting interests, is not included in the list. There is still a lot of interest in the north, and the *Tour de France*, which is the most famous cycle race in the world, although highly commercialised, is still one of the outstanding sporting events in France, and is either watched or followed by millions of French people. Great crowds turn out to see the cyclists race around 4000 kilometres through towns and villages. The rider with the leading time can always be spotted, because he wears a yellow vest, the famous *maillot jaune*. Although it is a French race, competitors of other nationalities take part, including Belgians, Dutch, Italians, Spanish, and British.

The Tour de France*: the world's greatest cycle race (Photo P. J. Downes)*

Skiing

Skiing is becoming very popular. It is France's fastest growing sport, and has been much encouraged in schools by winter sports classes, the *classes de neige*, which were begun in 1953.

Football

The most popular sport in France is now football. Professional football has two divisions, and many people play in the numerous amateur leagues. Apart from the league championship (the *Championnat de France*), the big event is the *Coupe de France*. French clubs participate in the European Cup and other European competitions, and France's international team, *L'Equipe de France*, compete in the World Cup.

Football matches are not normally played on Saturdays, but either on Sundays or midweek in the evenings. People prefer to sit down, even on the terraces, and unless there is a big crowd, anyone who stands up is not very popular if he is blocking the view of those behind!

Rugby

Both Rugby Union (*le Rugby à quinze*) and Rugby League (*le Rugby à treize*) are played in France, and are particularly popular in the south and south-west.

A local football match being played in Orleans (Photo La République du Centre)

Fishing

France has over three and a half million fishermen, and this is probably one of the most popular out-door pastimes, although not everybody is officially registered.

Shooting

Over two million people have licences for shooting, (*la chasse* in French does not mean 'big game hunting', but refers to game birds), and probably a lot more practice the sport unofficially!

Boules or *pétanque*

Different forms of bowls are played all over France, often on the village square, or on any open piece of ground. The bowls, which are usually made of solid steel, are thrown rather than rolled.

A game of pétanque
(Photo P. J. Downes)

Pelote

This is the native sport of the Basques, in the south-west of France (and also in Spain), and is played with a hard ball, which is knocked against a wall either by the hand or by a glove with a kind of basket attached to it.

L'Equipe

Most of these sports are regularly reported in the popular French sports paper, *L'Equipe*, which appears every day, as well as in a number of other sports papers and magazines which are either weekly or monthly.

Food

Good food and fine wines are part of the French way of life, and France prides herself on her tradition of good eating which goes back over 500 years. The French more than any other nation have raised cooking (*la cuisine*) to the status of an art.

Each area of France has its own special dishes, which are not only served in the home, but are also available in the local restaurants.

It is not surprising that a lot of the terms for food and cooking in many other languages are based on French words. Even the word 'chef' is short for the French *'chef de cuisine'*.

Those people who appreciate the finer points of the art of eating well are called *gastronomes* or *gourmets* (not to be confused with *gourmand*, which means 'greedy'.)

French people generally eat with their fork in the right hand, putting down their knife once they have used it for cutting meat etc.

Meat is usually served separately from vegetables, which are often a course in their own right.

Characteristics of French cooking

French meals tend to be less stodgy than in many countries, with more vegetables; fruit and cheese are more usual than puddings.

Garlic is used a good deal in cooking, especially in the south, to bring out the flavour of the food.

In northern France, butter is used a lot in cooking: in the south olive oil is used, and this tends to make the meals there 'heavier'.

French chefs make a speciality of their sauces, which are used rather than gravy, and these add greatly to the flavour of the dishes with which they are served. Many of the top restaurants employ a special chef just to take charge of the sauces, some of which he often creates himself.

Breakfast is served
(Photo P. J. Downes)

Breakfast (*le petit déjeuner*)

This is usually the simplest and quickest of French meals. It normally consists of:

A bowl of coffee, usually white (*café au lait*).
(Some people prefer tea or chocolate.)
Bread or *croissants*, with butter, and sometimes jam.

Although this is the traditional French breakfast it is by no means uniform, and those people who like something more substantial might have an egg, usually either boiled or fried.

Lunch (*le déjeuner*)

Lunch has traditionally been a two-hour break in France, so that people had time to go home for a full meal. Although some banks and large companies are trying to cut this down, there are still many firms and shops which close from 12 noon until 2 p.m. Unless they live a long way from work, in the past people have always liked to return home for this important family meal, often consisting of three or four courses. Nowadays, however, many people eat at their place of work or in a nearby restaurant.

Le goûter

This is an afternoon snack usually for children, who are often given a cup of chocolate and perhaps some bread etc. Adults normally take a *goûter* only if they are visiting friends; otherwise they either do without, or have a quick coffee.

Dinner (*le dîner*)

Dinner is usually the largest and longest meal of the day, as well as the main event of the evening, when all the family gather together to enjoy the meal and talk about the happenings of the day.

Before dinner, people often drink an *apéritif*, which is usually a wine, such as *Cinzano* or *Dubonnet*. The purpose of this is to stimulate the appetite, as well as to induce a mood of relaxation before the meal.

Wine, usually a good table wine, is served with the meal. Vintage wines are only for special occasions, and for those who can afford them.

After the meal coffee is usually served, either *café nature* (black coffee), or *café crème* (white coffee). This is often followed by a *digestif*, a drink such as brandy (*cognac*) etc.

Wine (*le vin*)

France is rightly famous for the quality and variety of the wine she produces. Wine is drunk all over France by rich and poor alike. Local *vin ordinaire* (ordinary table wine with no special label) is very cheap and drunk in considerable quantities.

Gathering grapes (Photo French Government Tourist Office)

Because wine is drunk with meals (children often drink it watered down), French people do not always realise how much alcohol they are consuming. This is perhaps why the consumption of alcohol in France is higher than in any other country in the world.

The type and quality of wine depend on three factors: the type of grape used (there are hundreds of varieties but only some two dozen in regular use in France); the type of soil and climatic conditions; the method of production from the time the grape is picked to the final bottling and storage. Every vineyard produces wine with its own particular flavour and characteristics. The secrets of their production are closely guarded.

Basically three qualities of wine are produced:

1. **Vin de pays** – usually a cheap local wine which is often blended, but which nevertheless passes a test of minimum quality and alcoholic strength.

2. **VDQS (Vin délimité de qualité supérieure)** – a wine of better quality, usually produced from grapes of a particular area though often blended.

3. **Appellation contrôlée** – Wine bearing this label has a government guarantee, not only of origin but also of quality. These wines, about fifteen per cent of the total annual production, are produced from grapes of a particular named and well-defined area and are made to very exacting

CHAMPAGNE

ALSACE

VAL DE LOIRE

MUSCADET   ANJOU

TOURAINE

BOURGOGNE

CÔTE DE NUITS

CÔTE DE BEAUNE

JURA

MACONNAIS

BEAUJOLAIS

COGNAC

BORDEAUX

MÉDOC

GRAVES St ÉMILION

BARSAC

SAUTERNES

SAVOIE

CÔTES DU RHÔNE

CHATEAUNEUF
DU PAPE

ARMAGNAC

LANGUEDOC

MINERVOIS

CORBIÈRES

ROUSSILLON

CÔTES DE PROVENCE

CORSE

*France's wine growing areas (Photo
Food and Wine from France)*

standards (now that we are in the Common Market we have
to observe these standards as well.) Wines in this class will
come almost exclusively from the classic wine-producing
areas of France, the most famous being: Bordeaux, Burgundy,
Beaujolais, Champagne, the Loire, the Rhône, and Alsace.

REGIONS	SOME EXAMPLES OF THE MOST COMMON NAMES YOU MAY FIND
BORDEAUX	Red: *Médoc, Saint – Emilion* White: *Graves, Sauternes, Barsac*
BURGUNDY	White: *Chablis, Mâcon* Red: *Nuits-St.-Georges, Beaune, Pommard*
BEAUJOLAIS	Red. *Moulin à Vent, Fleurie*
CÔTES DU RHÔNE	Red: *Châteauneuf du Pape, Hermitage* Rosé (pink): *Tavel*
CÔTES DE PROVENCE	Red: (V.D.Q.S.) *Pradel*
VAL DE LOIRE	Red: *Chinon* White: *Muscadet, Vouvray* Rosé: *Rosé d'Anjou*
ALSACE	White: *Riesling, Muscat*
CHAMPAGNE	Famous sparkling wine, e.g. *Moët et Chandon*
ROUSSILLON	Red and white table wines, e.g. *Banyuls, Rivesaltes*
COGNAC	Brandy, e.g. *Courvoisier, Martell*

Bordeaux   Burgundy and Beaujolais

Côtes du Rhône   Provence   Loire

Alsace   Champagne   Languedoc-Roussillon

One easy way of identifying French wine is by the shape of the bottle

Cheese (*le fromage*)

France's cheeses (Photo Food and Wine from France)

1. Mimolette
2. Boulette d'Avesnes
3. Rollet
4. Petit Saint-Paulin
5. Maroilles
6. Bondon
7. Boulette d'Avesnes
8. Cœur de Bray
9. Camembert
10. Fromage frais aromatisé
11. Fromage frais
12. Brie de Meaux
13. Saint-Paulin
14. Saint-Paulin
15. Pont l'Evêque
16. Pont l'Evêque
17. Saint-Paulin
18. Camembert
19. Livarot
20. Saint-Maure
21. Epoisses
22. Brie
23. Époisses
24. Carré de l'Est
25. Munster Géromé
26. Munster Géromé
27. Epoisses
28. Bleu de Bresse
29. Munster Géromé
30. Munster Géromé
31. Chaource
32. Gruyère de Comté
33. Bleu de Bresse
34. Bleu de Bresse
35. Crottin de Chavignol
36. Pyramide du Poitou
37. Curé Nantais
38. Saint-Nectaire
39. Pyramide du Poitou
40. Bleu de Bresse
41. Cantal
42. Fourme d'Ambert
43. Camembert
44. Fourme d'Ambert
45. Emmental
46. Beaufort
47. Saint Marcellin
48. Tomme de Savoie
49. Bleu d'Auvergne
50. Bleu des Caussers
51. Roquefort
52. Roquefort
53. Saint–Paulin
54. Fromage des Pyrénées
55. Rigottes
56. Fromage fondu aux raisins
57. Banon de Provence
58. Poivre d'Ane
59. Niolo

France produces almost as great a variety of cheese as of wines: over 300 different cheeses, and a total of over 650 000 tonnes of cheese a year, much of it for export.

Some cheeses are made from cow's milk, some from sheep's milk and some from goat's milk.

Among the more famous French cheeses are:

Camembert: a strong flavoured (and strong smelling!) cheese, made in Normandy
Brie: a strong cheese made in north-west France
Roquefort: is made in southern France from sheep's milk
Gruyère: a mild cheese made in eastern France

Restaurants and cafés

Some of the finest restaurants in the world are in France. They are graded in the Michelin Guide by a series of stars, but only very few have three stars, and these are world-famous. People travel considerable distances for the experience of eating in them.

One does not have to go to one of these great restaurants in order to get an excellent meal in France. There are thousands of small restaurants in towns and villages throughout France where there is a very high standard of cooking, often undertaken by the owner (*le patron*) himself.

Good food is appreciated by everybody in all walks of life in France: among the best value meals in France are those served in the *relais routiers*, the restaurants for long-distance lorry drivers! These can be used by other people as well as by lorrry-drivers.

If one just wants a drink or a coffee, it is as well to know that prices can vary enormously for exactly the same thing. The big restaurant on

What's on the menu?
(Photo P. J. Downes)

Bon Appétit! *A typical French restaurant (Photo P. J. Downes)*

a boulevard or main street usually charges a lot more than a smaller restaurant or *café-bar* in a side street. There are often three different prices for the same drink, even within each restaurant or café;

1. sitting on the *terrasse* (the most expensive)
2. sitting inside (less expensive)
3. sitting or standing at the bar (the cheapest).

So if all that is wanted is a quick drink, the cheapest way is to have it at the bar, because the same drink can cost almost twice as much on the *terrasse*!

Tips (*pourboires*)

It is usual (even expected) for people to leave a tip, even after merely having a quick drink. This is normally between ten and fifteen per cent of the cost of the meal or drink. In many bars and restaurants, the menu includes a notice: '*service compris*'. This means that the money for a tip has already been added to the bill, so it is not necessary to tip again (although the waiter is unlikely to protest if he gets a tip as well!)

Shopping

Department stores (*les grands magasins*)

In the larger towns there are a number of department stores (*grands magasins*), which are similar to department stores anywhere. Stores such as the *Galeries Lafayette*, *Grande Samaritaine* and *Au Printemps* in Paris are among the most famous; others like the *Monoprix* (known in some parts of France as *Prisunic* or *Midiprix*) have branches throughout the country.

Supermarkets (*les supermarchés*)

The 1950s saw the introduction of a new kind of shopping, in the form of the self-service supermarkets (*supermarchés*), of which the largest is the *Carrefour* chain of nearly 2000 shops (about three-quarters of all France's supermarkets). To a large extent these were a product not only of the increasing wealth of France and the growing spending power of ordinary French people, but also of American sales techniques which were studied (sometimes in America) by large numbers of people employed in the retail trade. The success of these new supermarkets was based on a number of factors: self-service selling methods allowed the number of staff and staff wages to be cut, and bulk buying meant lower costs, which, together with aggressive sales techniques, led to rapid turnover. So by the late 1970s a quarter of all the food sold in France was sold in supermarkets.

Hypermarkets (*les hypermarchés*)

A recent further development, which has grown out of the success of the *supermarchés*, has been the appearance of the *hypermarchés*

Left, the Monoprix, *a popular department store which has branches all over France (Photo P. J. Downes)*

Right, a hypermarket: this scene shows why they are often referred to as Les grandes surfaces *(Photo P. J. Downes)*

(hypermarkets). These are giant new stores, using the supermarket techniques, but are much larger. They are usually situated on the outskirts of towns, with plenty of space for parking cars, so that the housewife can buy in bulk, often doing the week's shopping on a single visit. The first hypermarket was opened in 1963 near Orly, to the south of Paris, and the present number of around 400 is still growing. The *Carrefour* hypermarket outside Marseilles is the largest store in Europe, with 22 000 square metres of selling space, which is as big as a four-hectare field.

Effects on small shopkeepers The introduction of supermarkets and hypermarkets had a disastrous effect on the traditional small French shop-keepers, who found they could no longer compete. Many were driven out of business altogether, but some of the more astute realised that whilst they could not compete on the same lines as the supermarkets, the answer lay in trying to offer specialised services and types of goods which were not offered by the supermarkets: personal service and deliveries, certain types of luxury goods, repair services, etc. By adapting in this way, many small shop-keepers have been able to survive, but the general trend is still towards a gradual but steady cutting down of the number of small shops, and many thousands are driven out of business every year.

High street shops

A horse butcher's

Along the high street of the average French suburb or village the same sort of shops etc. appear as in most countries, yet in many ways they have distinctively French characteristics. The traditional small shops which have been the basis of French shopping for centuries are still to be found in most French towns:

La boucherie is the butcher's shop in which raw but not cooked meat is sold. French butchers normally cut most of the fat off the meat before weighing it. *La boucherie chevaline* is a butcher's shop selling horse-meat, which is commonly eaten as a cheaper meat by French people. A *boucherie chevaline* can usually be picked out by its sign, which is a model of a horse's head, often painted gold, displayed outside above the shop door.

La charcuterie sells cooked meats and pork meat products, including various kinds of *pâté* (meat paste), ham, sausages, salami etc.

La poissonnerie is the fishmonger's and sells a variety of shell fish as well as wet fish.

La boulangerie is the bakery, where all sorts and sizes of loaves are sold, as well as the *croissants* (which are crescent-shaped and made of flaky bread) commonly eaten for breakfast. The *boulangerie* opens very early in the morning, so that people can buy their bread and *croissants* freshly cooked for breakfast. It closes from 2.00 p.m. until 4.00 p.m. so that new bread can be made for people to buy fresh for the evening

Unloading meat at a charcuterie
(Photo H. Jaeger – DF)

meal. Nearly all French bread is produced by the local baker, and not mass-produced or steam-baked as is much of our bread.

La pâtisserie is the pastry shop, which sells all sorts of pastries (*pâtisseries*), cakes (*gâteaux*), fruit tarts (*tartes aux fruits*), and sweet bread (*brioches*). A pleasant Sunday morning job is going to the *pâtisserie* to choose pastries to eat with the Sunday lunch.

L'épicerie is the grocer's shop, which sells green groceries, such as fruit and vegetables, as well as the ordinary groceries, i.e. coffee, sugar, flour, tinned goods, etc. It also combines the role of off-licence, and is the main place for buying wines and spirits.

The épicerie *(Photo J. P. Hachet – DF)*

La crémerie is the dairy shop, which sells cream, butter, eggs and yoghurt, as well as milk, which in France is not usually delivered to the house.

Alimentation is the sign for a general store selling all sorts of food and groceries, and is the sort of shop often found in small villages.

La pharmacie is the chemist's shop, and can be spotted by the sign of a green cross, which is usually illuminated so that it can be easily picked out.

La quincaillerie is the hardware shop.

La cordonnerie is the shoe-repairer's or cobbler's shop.

Le bar-tabac is a bar which sells not only alcoholic drinks and coffee, cigarettes and tobacco, but also postage stamps. A red carrot-shaped sign outside distinguishes it from the ordinary bar, which is not licensed to sell stamps or cigarettes.

In villages or localities which have no public toilet, it is quite normal to use the toilet in a local bar or café, provided one leaves a small tip!

Le marché Many small towns and large villages have their own market, which is very much a traditional part of French life. Housewives often do much of their shopping here for fresh fruit and vegetables, which they expect to be able to pick up and choose for themselves. Prices are usually cheaper and the goods often fresher than in the shops.

The local market (Photo P. J. Downes)

Other high street institutions

Le bureau de poste Here one can buy the usual things one gets in a post office: stamps, telegrams etc. In all French post offices, all the current French stamps are on display. At most post offices, either inside or just outside, there is a telephone box or *kiosque téléphonique*.

*A French telephone
(Photo P. J. Downes)*

A kiosque téléphonique
(Photo P. J. Downes)

La mairie or *hôtel de ville*, is the town hall. This usually has the red, white and blue French tricolour outside, and is where most of the local authority business is carried out.

The hôtel de ville

Le commissariat de police is the police station, not to be confused with the *gendarmerie*, which is the local militia post. Both the *agents de police* (policemen, known in slang as *flics*) and the *gendarmes* (militia)

A French policeman on traffic duty
(Photo Affaires Étrangères)

carry revolvers, but the uniform of the *agents de police* is dark blue, while the *gendarme*'s uniform is khaki. Traffic police usually wear white gloves and carry a white baton which they use to signal to the traffic, and also a whistle which they blow frequently to attract drivers' attention to their signals.

La banque There are usually branches of one or two famous banks, such as *Crédit Lyonnais*, or the Savings Bank (*Caisse d'Epargne*), in any high street. These usually contain a *bureau de change*, where foreign money or traveller's cheques can be changed. Some travel agents (*agents de voyages*) also have a *bureau de change*, which is indicated by a large sign: *CHANGE*.

Transport and communications

France has a complex system of roads and railways, a national air-line, and an expanding system of waterways.

Road transport and motoring

France has one of the most highly developed road systems in the world; of the 700 000 km of roads, 80 000 km are *routes nationales*, (like our 'A' roads), which the French call 'N' roads. Local roads are called 'D' roads (*routes départementales*).

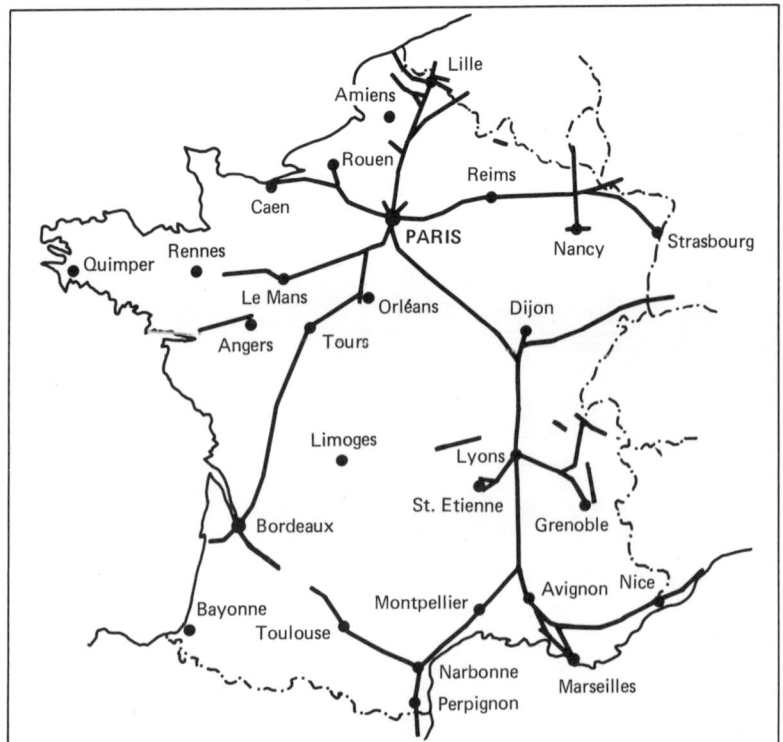

French motorways

France has over 4000 km of *autoroutes* (motorways or freeways) or 'A' roads. These form a direct link from Lille in the north, through Paris, to the Mediterranean at Marseilles.

French *autoroutes* are toll roads, i.e. one has to pay at one of the *péages*, or toll stops. The amount to be paid varies according to how far one travels.

On French roads, one must not only drive on the right hand side, but give way to all traffic coming from the right: this is the meaning of the sign '*priorité à droite*', (i.e. give priority to all traffic coming from the right, or from roads on the right).

French railways

French railways are a state-controlled industry under the *Société des Chemins de Fer Français* (*SNCF*), which was set up in 1937. There are 37 700 km of railways, of which more than 10 000 km are electrified. All the main lines radiate out from Paris, which is the heart of the French rail and transport system.

Among the high-speed trains, probably the best known are: the record-breaking *Mistral*, which averages 120 km/hr for the Paris-Lyons run, i.e. 572 km in five hours, and *Le Capitole*, which has reached a top speed of 200 km/hr between Paris and Toulouse.

A high speed train or *TGV* (*Train à grande vitesse*) was introduced in 1981, with a maximum travelling speed of 260 km/hr, but it is capable of an incredible 380 km/hr.

A new experimental overhead *aérotrain*, running on a cushion of air, has been produced, and may well be the train of the future.

The new high speed train (TGV) (Photo SNCF – Broncard)

Air transport

This is dominated by the French national airline, *Air France*, and its domestic subsidiary, *Air Inter.*

In 1970, French airlines carried twenty times as many passengers, and four times as much goods as in 1960 and in 1980 Air France alone carried nearly 11 million passengers (5 million more than in 1970).

By 1985 Charles de Gaulle Airport is expected to handle 60 million passengers, and employ a staff of 70 000 people.

The next most important airports are at Nice, Marseilles and Lyons.

Water transport

France's rivers and ports are linked by a series of canals to form a system of inland waterways. These are an important part of France's system of transporting goods and freight. Eight per cent of France's freight traffic is carried by water on the large self-propelled barges (*péniches*), which are often linked in strings of five, carrying a total of up to 3000 tonnes. In 1968, waterways carried six times more goods than in 1957, and half as much again by 1975. In 1976, 12 000 million tonnes per km were carried on a network of nearly 7000 km.

This system is intended to link the Mediterranean with the Atlantic and the North Sea, and by linking with the Rhine, to join up with the German and European inland waterways and the Baltic, to the north.

Canals and navigable waterways

Among the important links are:

The *Canal du Midi* (in south-west France) which links the Mediterranean and its busy port of Marseilles with the Atlantic and the Atlantic port of Bordeaux.

The *Loire Latéral Canal* (in central France) which links the Rhône and the Mediterranean with Paris and the Seine. These in turn are linked up with Rouen and the Atlantic, the Channel, and with the industrial regions of the north of France.

The *St Quentin Canal* (in the north) which links Paris and the northern industrial towns with the highly-developed waterway system of the Benelux countries of Holland, Belgium and Luxembourg.

The *Marne-Rhine Canal* linking Paris with the Rhine and the German waterway system, which will link the Rhine and Main with the Danube and Eastern Europe.

The *Rhône-Rhine Canal* (due for completion in 1985) which will create a 370 km link between the Saône and the Rhine, making a single 1800 km waterway for water traffic to travel directly between Marseilles and the Mediterranean and Rotterdam and the North Sea.

This type of water transport for large commercial cargoes is used on

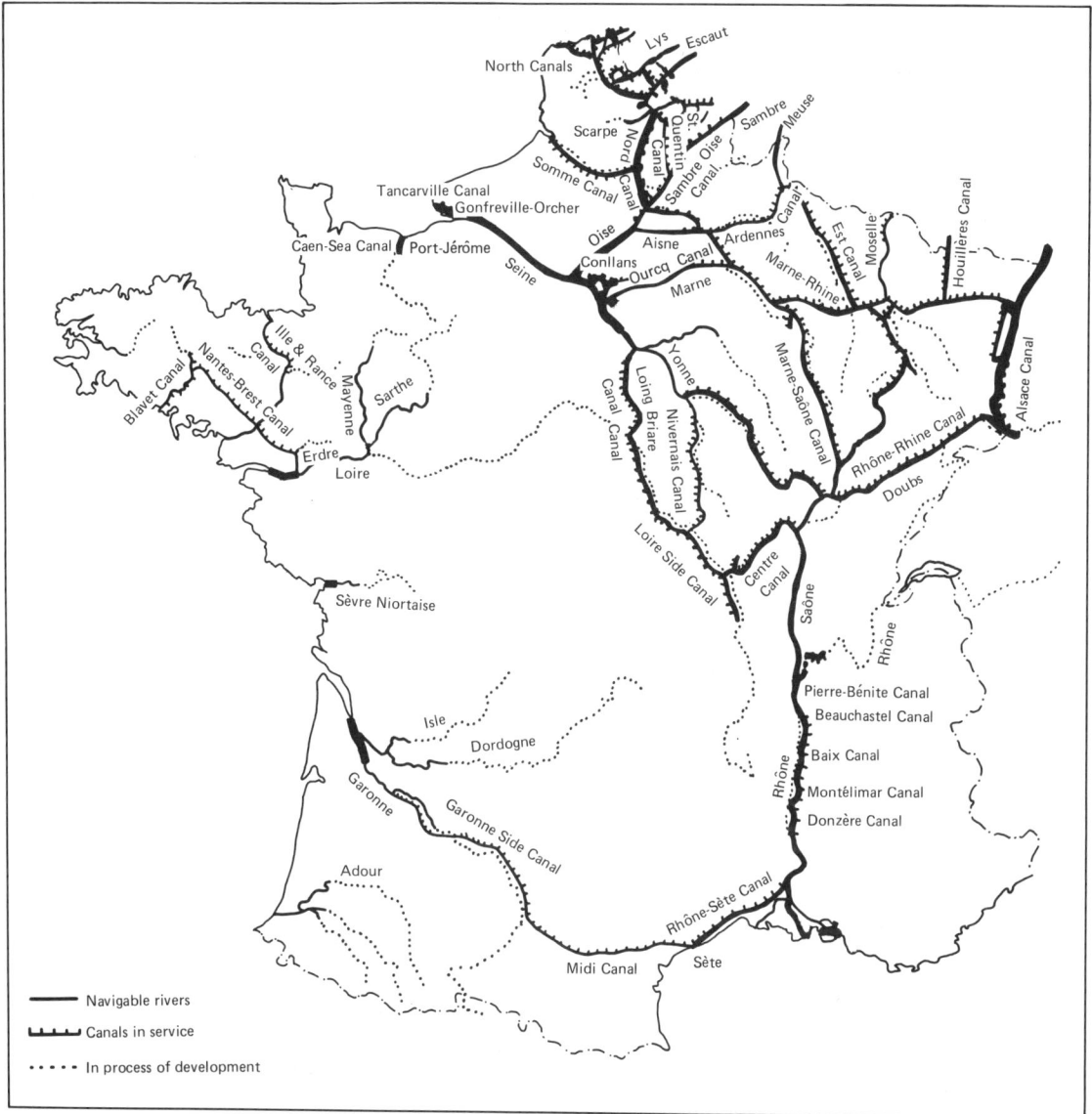

French canals and waterways

Map labels: North Canals, Lys, Escaut, Scarpe, St. Quentin Canal, Sambre, Meuse, Somme Canal, Nord Canal, Sambre Oise Canal, Tancarville Canal, Gonfreville-Orcher, Oise, Aisne, Ardennes, Est Canal, Moselle, Houillères Canal, Caen-Sea Canal, Port-Jérôme, Seine, Conflans, Ourcq Canal, Marne, Marne-Rhine, Alsace Canal, Ille & Rance Canal, Mayenne, Sarthe, Yonne, Marne-Saône Canal, Blavet Canal, Nantes-Brest Canal, Erdre, Loire, Canal Canal, Loing Briare Canal, Nivernais Canal, Rhône-Rhine Canal, Doubs, Loire Side Canal, Centre Canal, Sèvre Niortaise, Saône, Rhône, Pierre-Bénite Canal, Beauchastel Canal, Isle, Dordogne, Baix Canal, Montélimar Canal, Donzère Canal, Garonne, Garonne Side Canal, Rhône, Adour, Rhône-Sète Canal, Midi Canal, Sète

Legend:
— Navigable rivers
ⱢⱢⱢⱢ Canals in service
· · · · · In process of development

a wide scale in Germany and the Benelux countries, and increasingly in France as a result of the various developments which are now in hand.

Advantages

Waterway transport has many advantages:
1. Fuel and running costs are low, at a time when oil and other fuels are very expensive.
2. The huge 'European' barges (*péniches*) of some 1300 tonnes can carry large quantities of cargo, as their size is not limited in the way that lorries are limited by roads and trains by rails.
3. This form of transport causes very little pollution.

SECTION C: PARIS

Hôtel de Ville, Paris (Photo French Government Tourist Office)

The importance of Paris

As well as being the capital of France, Paris is widely considered to be one of the most beautiful and exciting cities in Europe. People flock to Paris for its many places of interest and tourist attractions, which include not only night clubs and sights such as the Eiffel Tower, but also theatres, museums and art galleries.

But Paris is much more than just a tourist attraction for foreigners; for Parisians it is a working city. It is not only the political capital of France and, therefore, the seat of French government, but also the administrative, economic, industrial and cultural centre of France. It is moreover by far the largest city, where nearly ten million people live, work, go to school and spend their leisure hours. It is divided into twenty *arrondissements:* each with its own *mairie*, but all under the overall control of the *hôtel de ville*.

44

Transport   Although Paris is not situated at the geographical centre of France, it is very much at the centre of France in nearly every other sense. If you think of the transport system of a country as its economic arteries, then Paris is like the beating heart of France, for it lies at the centre of the French transport system: the motorways, main roads, railways, air services (as well as a good deal of its water transport) are all centred on Paris, and if 'all roads lead to Paris', it is because so many people have wanted and needed to go there – and still do.

Centralisation   The role Paris plays today in the life of France results from centuries of being at the heart of nearly all important aspects of French life. This was due to a policy known as 'centralisation', by which as much of French life as possible was directed from Paris. The effect of this has been that Paris has dominated French life to a far greater extent than is the case of capital cities in most other countries. To stay or live in Paris today still gives you very much the feeling of being at the centre of things as far as France is concerned.

The people of Paris

Dominance of Paris   It is when we look at the population of Paris and compare it with the rest of France that we can appreciate the dominant position of Paris and how far it has an unhealthy effect on the whole of the French economy. Although just over two and a quarter million people live in Paris itself, nearly eleven million people live in the Paris Region. This means that *almost one Frenchman in every five lives in or near Paris.*

Below, a Paris traffic policeman helping tourists

Paris – the heart of France (Photo Camberoque – DF)

Rapid growth It is a region in which the population has expanded enormously during the last few years: between 1946 and 1975, the population of the Paris Region increased by three and a quarter million, though this expansion now appears to have slowed down. Yet the fact remains that in Paris over eighteen per cent of all French people live in

The new Paris emerges – with traditional Paris in the background (Photo Atelier XIII – Semea XV)

an area of just over two per cent of the land; and there are nearly twice as many people per hectare as in London, with less than half the area of parks that exist in London or New York. The effect of this rapid increase has been firstly to strain the resources of Paris in accommodating all these extra people. Secondly, because Paris has grown much faster than the rest of France, it has meant that a large number of people were leaving other parts of France to come to live and work in Paris. So problems were created both for Paris and for the rest of the country.

All this explains why in recent years the government has made strenuous efforts to reduce this dominance by encouraging growth in other parts of France.

Position: Paris and the Seine

Paris owes its existence, like many towns, to its position on a river. It stands on the Seine, close to where it is joined by its tributary, the Marne. (The ancient coat of arms of Paris includes a ship, which shows how important the river and its trade have been throughout the history of Paris.) The Seine still plays an important role today both for business and pleasure. It is a busy working river, with many big barges (*péniches*) carrying goods and materials to and from Paris, which is the largest river port in France. For Paris is not only connected by the Seine to the sea 240 km away, but also to other parts of France and Europe by the highly developed system of waterways formed by the network of rivers and canals, which is in the process of being developed futher.

The coat of arms of Paris (Photo P. J. Downes)

FLUCTUAT NEC MERGITUR

Paris, showing the Ile-de-la-Cité, the Ile Saint-Louis, and the bridges
(Photo Sodel – M. Brigaud)

A bateau-mouche *on the Seine*
(Photo P. J. Downes)

The river also provides the means of showing tourists the sights of Paris. A trip on the river in one of the *bateaux mouches* gives the tourist a chance to see the well-known landmarks from rather an unusual angle. Some of the *bateaux mouches* offer a meal as part of the trip, but beware of the price!

Bridges Although Paris is cut in two by the Seine, getting across the city presents no real problem because there are so many bridges over the river. These are often ancient and elegant bridges which are an essential part of the Paris scene: the most ancient of Paris bridges is the Pont Neuf (meaning 'New Bridge')! As well as the bridges over the river, the river is crossed by the *métro* which goes under it at a number of points.

Paris and its past

Romans Paris takes its name from that of a Celtic tribe called the *Parisii*, who lived there before the arrival of the Romans. When the Romans came in 52 BC, France became the Roman province of Gaul, of which Paris was the capital (its Roman name was *Lutetia*, or *Lutèce* in modern French.) You can still see some Roman remains in Paris, notably the *Arènes de Lutèce* (or 'Arena of Lutetia').

Islands The original historic centre of Paris was on one of the two islands in the middle of the Seine, the Ile de la Cité. The other island is the Ile Saint-Louis, which is made up of two small islands joined together in 1614. In spite of all the modern developments in Paris, the Ile Saint-Louis is still full of character and remains one of the most peaceful parts of the city. Nearly all its buildings date back to the seventeenth century when it was one of the most fashionable parts of Paris in which to live.

Middle Ages In the Middle Ages Paris was one of the great European centres of scholarship and religion, attracting scholars and students from all over Europe, including Britain, to study at the University of Paris. One of the medieval colleges was the Sorbonne (founded in 1253), which still survives today.

Royal palaces As the historic capital of France, Paris was also the seat of the French kings and their courts. Several royal palaces still survive in and around Paris: in Paris itself are the Louvre and the Palais Royal; outside Paris are the palaces of Versailles (the great achievement of Louis XIV), and Fontainebleau.

Paris today

Left Bank (*Rive Gauche*) and the Latin Quarter

On the *Rive Gauche* (the Left Bank, or South Bank) is the Latin Quarter (*le Quartier Latin*), centred on the University of Paris.

The Latin Quarter got its name because the common language of scholars and students in the Middle Ages was Latin, and this was the district or quarter where Latin was spoken. Nowadays it is one of the most lively and picturesque parts of Paris: with its ancient buildings and its narrow, medieval streets, usually crowded with students of all colours and nationalities, it has kept much of the character it has had since the Middle Ages. There are many colourful cafés and restaurants, both on the main streets such as the Boulevard Saint-Michel (known to students as the 'Boul' Mich' ') and the Boulevard Saint-Germain, and on the little side streets.

The Latin Quarter also contains many buildings of later date, such as the Palais du Luxembourg (the seat of the French Senate), the gardens of which are much frequented by students; and the Panthéon, where many of France's famous dead are buried (rather like Westminster Abbey in Britain).

Also on the Left Bank is the Montparnasse area, the home of many of the large number of French and foreign artists living and working in Paris, which has traditionally been, and still is, one of the art centres of the world.

University

The University of Paris is one of the oldest in Europe and is the mother university of Oxford and Cambridge: in the early Middle Ages Brtish students used to travel to Paris to study at the university, but because of wars they decided to migrate back to Britain, where they congregated at Oxford, and later at Cambridge. The original buildings

The Panthéon (Photo French Government Tourist Office)

of the Sorbonne are no longer standing, but today the university is larger and more flourishing than ever.

Paris continues to attract students from all parts of the world, just as it has done for nearly 800 years. In fact the university has become so large that it has had to be split into a number of smaller universities, including that on a new site outside Paris at Nanterre to the north.

To get an impression of the number of students in Paris (there are in fact over a quarter of a million), we have to realise that it is greater than the whole population of many quite important towns. Many students are housed in the hostels of the international student communities such as those of the *Cité Universitaire* at Sceaux and also at Antony, suburbs to the south of Paris.

The Sorbonne (Photo E. Revault)

Grandes écoles

As well as the university itself, Paris has also a number of so-called *grandes écoles*, (see under 'Education') e.g. the *Ecole Normale Supérieure* (for the training of top-level teachers), the *Ecole Polytechnique* (for high-level technologists) and the *Ecole Nationale d'Administration* (for the training of senior civil servants).

Schools

Also in the Latin Quarter are some of Paris's most famous schools, including the *Lycée Henri IV*, the *Lycée Louis-le-Grand*, and the *Lycée Saint-Louis*, where some of France's most famous men were educated.

Right Bank (*Rive Droite*) and the business area

Montmartre The original artists' quarter was in Montmartre, the hill on the north part of the Right Bank, which is surmounted by the mosque-like church of the Sacré-Cœur. This was the quarter or district frequented by artists and painters at the end of last century, and scenes from its night clubs and other aspects of its life have been made famous by the paintings of Toulouse-Lautrec. However this area has now been largely deserted by the real artists, leaving behind the night clubs and other tourist haunts.

Business centre The Right Bank (*Rive Droite*) is the centre of much of Paris's business and commercial life. Here are to be found many of the great business and financial institutions: the *Bourse* (the Paris Stock Exchange); the head offices of many of France's banks and most important companies, and the offices of most of France's largest national newspapers, 70 per cent of which are based in Paris. These include *Le Figaro*, *Le Monde* (both daily papers) and the weekly *Paris Match*, an outstanding photographic news magazine, which employs some of the world's highest-paid photographers.

Shops On the Right Bank are some of France's best known shops, such as the department stores *Galeries Lafayette* and the *Grande Samaritaine*, and also the headquarters of famous fashion designers (*couturiers*), such as Dior, Balmain, Lapidus, Courrèges, etc., leaders of the world's fashions. The displays of new collections are greeted like theatrical events and eagerly reported in the press all over the world.

Boulevards On the Right Bank are many of the elegant boulevards – the straight, broad, tree-lined streets or avenues, built during the nineteenth century by a Baron Haussmann, in order to allow soldiers to move freely in the event of uprisings or revolution. (He also created a number of open spaces, including the parks of the Bois de Boulogne and the Bois de Vincennes.) Perhaps the most elegant of all is the Avenue des Champs-Elysées, which is a very wide avenue, lined with trees. It is the site of a number of prestigious offices of companies, banks, airlines etc., as well as cafés, restaurants and cinemas. It is fashionable to while away the hours on the terrace of one of the many cafés of the Champs-Elysées. This can be an expensive pleasure, however, for the cost of a coffee or lemonade here is almost as much as a light meal in more modest surroundings!

The Champs-Elysées, which was constructed as a triumphal way, leads straight to the Place Charles de Gaulle. This was formerly known

Montmartre and the Sacré-Cœur (Photo Interphotothèque)

◀ *The Place Charles de Gaulle, showing the Arc de Triomphe and the elegant boulevards radiating outwards from it (Photo Interphotothèque)*

as the Place de l'Etoile, because it is the central point of a number of boulevards, which radiate outwards in the shape of a star (*étoile*). At the centre of this square is the Arc de Triomphe, which is a triumphal archway constructed on the orders of Napoleon in honour of the French Army, whose exploits in Napoleon's great battles are carved on it. (There is no mention of his defeats!) Unfortunately Napoleon never lived to see it, though his body passed under it on the way to its final resting place in Les Invalides, where you can still see his tomb today.

At the Arc de Triomphe is the Tomb of the Unknown Soldier, where a flame is kept perpetually alight to commemorate the French soldiers who were killed during the two World Wars. The Armistice Day ceremony is held here each year, just as the Champs-Elysées is the scene of military parades, such as that which celebrates the Liberation from German occupation.

Important buildings and places of interest

Notre-Dame de Paris

Situated on the Ile de la Cité, at the historic heart of the city, Notre-Dame is one of the great Gothic cathedrals of Europe, built between 1163 and 1345. Its beauty is enhanced by its position at the end of the island, where it seems almost to rise out of the water.

Notre-Dame de Paris

The Sainte-Chapelle

Also on the Ile de La Cité, built within the *Palais de Justice* (the Central Law Courts), on the site of the old Roman headquarters of Paris, the Sainte-Chapelle is a little jewel of medieval architecture which is often missed by foreign tourists, but much appreciated by Parisians. It is unique in that it is built on two levels, supported by slender Gothic pillars, and has some of the most beautiful medieval stained glass in France.

The Louvre

Although the original buildings date from an earlier period, this palace was the Paris residence of Louis XIV, who adapted and extended the earlier buildings. It was the seat of the Court, when the king was in Paris, although after his youth he spent more of his time at the even greater Palace of Versailles, a few kilometres to the south of Paris.

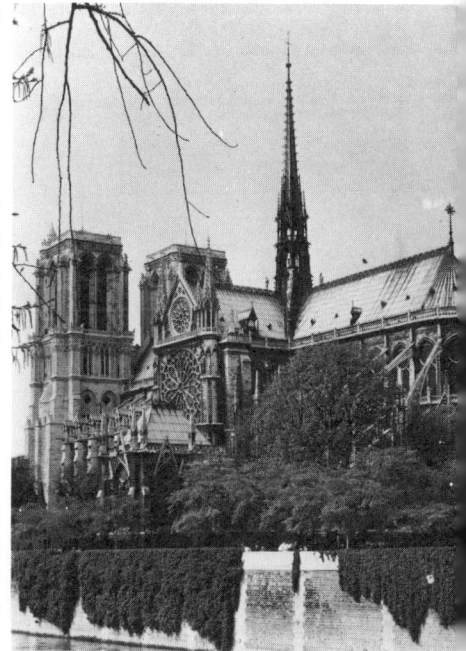

The *Conciergerie*

This is not a church but a medieval fortress which at the time of the French Revolution was the prison where many members of the aristocracy, including the Queen, Marie-Antoinette, were held before being beheaded by the guillotine!

Other important medieval buildings are the cathedral of Saint-Denis, the abbey of Saint Germain-des-Prés, and the churches of Saint Julien-le-Pauvre and Saint Séverin (both in the Latin Quarter).

An impressively large proportion of the buildings in the centre of Paris date either from the seventeenth century, or are built in the style of this period, when Paris was at the height of its glory as the capital of the richest and most powerful country in Europe. It is essentially this period which has stamped its grandiose and elegant style on the character of Paris as we know it today: it was not merely a display of wealth but an expression of good taste, style and moderation and all the qualities associated with this great period (the *Grande Epoque*) of French history, that was dominated by Louis XIV and his Court.

The *Opéra*

This is one of the most striking nineteenth-century buildings in Paris, and is not only the home of Grand Opera in Paris, but the scene of many spectacular gala performances attended by the president and important foreign guests.

Place de la Concorde

This is a famous square formerly known as the Place de la Révolution, as it was the site of the guillotine during the revolution, when so many members of the French aristocracy were beheaded.

Eiffel Tower (*la Tour Eiffel*)

This was built for an International Exhibition in 1889, when it was the world's tallest building (300 m tall, and weighing some 7000 tonnes), and was regarded as one of the wonders of the world. As well as being a tourist attraction, offering spectacular views over Paris, nowadays it houses a restaurant, a television aerial, and a meteorological laboratory. Fortunately a lift is provided (although some people prefer to test their leg muscles by climbing the stairs!)

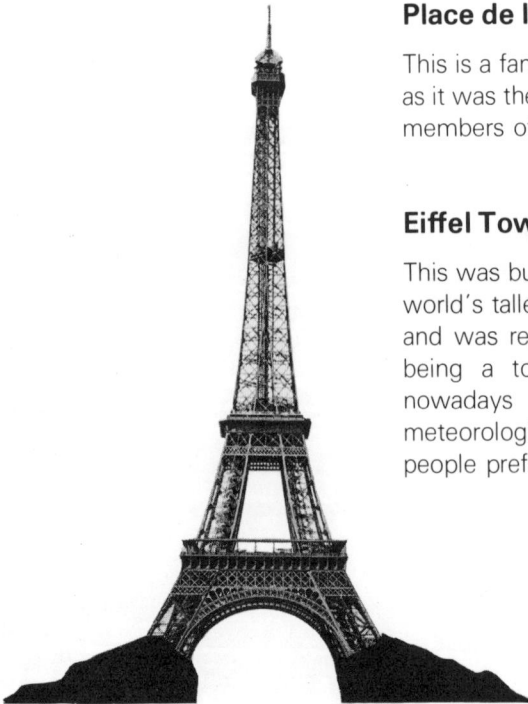

Les Halles *at Rungis (J. Pottier – DF)*

Working Paris

Industry

It is often forgotten that Paris is by far the largest centre of industry in France. About one quarter of French manufacturing industry is based in the Paris region, which provides jobs for nearly two million manual workers, plus thousands more technicians.

Examples of the kinds of industries in Paris are:

Metal based industries Car factories (e.g. the state-controlled firms of Renault and Citroën), machine tools, aeroplanes, electrical, electronics and telecommunications.

Food Industry Centred on the great market of *Les Halles* at Rungis (on the southern outskirts of Paris). In addition to the factories producing and processing different kinds of foods, Paris has many hotels and restaurants employing people in various jobs.

Luxury industries Paris is also famous for fashion design and is arguably the most important fashion centre in the world. Other luxury industries are furniture, jewellery and perfumes.

The Renault factory at Bellancourt, on the outskirts of Paris (Photo Renault)

L'Assemblée Nationale *in session*
(Photo Jean Louis NOU — DF)

Le Palais du Luxembourg, *home of
the French Senate*

Commerce

As well as the people involved in producing goods for sale many more thousands of people are employed in business or commercial jobs (i.e. office type jobs) concerned with the marketing of these products.

Government and administration

National government Just as Paris is the headquarters of so many industrial firms, it is also the centre of the national government and its many ministries, with their thousands of civil servants. (The French have their share of bureaucracy and red tape as well!) A number of these ministries are on or near the Place de la Concorde, whilst the French Foreign Ministry is on the Quai d'Orsay.

As the capital, Paris is the home of the President of the Republic, whose official residence is at the Elysée Palace, and of the French Parliament, with its two chambers: the National Assembly (*l'Assemblée Nationale*), which is housed in the Palais Bourbon, and the Senate (*le Sénat*), which is housed in the Luxembourg Palace (*le Palais du Luxembourg*), in the heart of the Latin Quarter.

Local government Thousands more people work for the local authorities, for Paris has the largest local authority in France, based on the *Hôtel de Ville,* and is headquarters of both a *département* and a region. Because of its size, Paris is divided into twenty *arrondissements*, or administrative districts, each with its own mayor and staff.

Many more jobs are provided by the various public services, such as banks, public transport etc.

Leisure and entertainment

Theatres

Paris has a wide variety of more than 60 theatres, including the state theatres such as the *Comédie Française* (which means theatre rather than comedy!), the *Opéra* (home of Grand Opera), and the *Opéra Comique,* as well as a large selection of commercial theatres and night clubs of all sorts. Most of the night clubs are very expensive and are largely frequented by tourists or businessmen.

Art

Paris has always been regarded as a world centre of the arts, and has about 80 museums and 200 art galleries, the most famous of which is perhaps the Louvre, formerly a royal palace, now the home of one of the greatest art collections in the world. Among its treasures is the

The Comédie Francaise *in one of Molière's comedies (Photo Bernand – Tourisme)*

Musée Carnavalet, with its collection of items relating to the history of Paris.

Music

Paris has a number of famous symphony orchestras, each giving regular concerts, in addition to a number of visiting orchestras from other countries. The Paris *Conservatoire* is one of the world's leading schools of music; since the Revolution it has been a centre for some of France's most brilliant composers, and like the *Ecole des Beaux Arts*, which is the school of Painting and Fine Arts, it attracts students from all over the world.

You can find out all the details about current programmes of theatres, concerts, exhibitions, etc., from *L'Officiel des Spectacles* and *Une Semaine de Paris – Pariscope*, which are booklets published each week, and can be bought from any newspaper stall or kiosk.

Books

Paris has a number of libraries of which the most important are the *Bibliothèque Nationale*, and the various university collections, including the Library of the Sorbonne. If you want to buy a book you can go to one of the many bookshops selling both new and second-hand books; or there is the pleasure of strolling along the quays (or *quais*) of the river and browsing at the stalls of the *bouquinistes*, with their second-hand books and prints of paintings.

Sport

Paris offers many sporting facilities and sports centres, including the modern stadium of the Parc des Princes, which will hold 50 000 spectators all seated and under cover. This is where the French Football Cup Final is played, usually attended by the President of the French Republic. The winners of this competition compete in the European Cup Winners' Cup.

The French Athletics Championships are staged at the Stade Colombes, just outside Paris, and the French Tennis Championship, which is a hard-court championship taking place just before Wimbledon, is held at the Stade Roland-Garros. There are a number of horse-racing courses, including those at Vincennes, Auteuil and Longchamp (which holds two of the most famous races in Europe: *Le Grand Prix de l'Arc de Triomphe* and *Le Grand Prix de Paris*.)

In the middle of July the great cycling race, the *Tour de France*, is held, and after winding through France completes its final stage in Paris.

Paris transport

The *RATP* (*Réseau Autonome des Transports Parisiens*)

In order to cope with its large population, Paris has a highly developed transport system, not only to move people and goods within the city, but also into and out of the city. The size of the task can be judged from the fact that the Paris Transport Authority, (the *RATP*) carries nearly five million people a day; over a million of these commute to and from the city centre. It is worth remembering that in France the evening rush hour begins at 6.00 p.m., due to the fact that Parisians, like most French people, have traditionally had a two-hour break for lunch. Yet in spite of the strain under which it operates, the public transport system has coped very efficiently, and services have even been modernised and expanded.

A Paris métro *station: Louvre (Photo Clausse – RATP)*

The *métro*

The *métro* (short for *métropolitain*), or underground railway, was opened in 1900 and is still the quickest way of getting around or across Paris. A network of some 500 *métro* stations (*stations de métro*) covers the whole of the Paris area, and links up with the main line services, the *SNCF* (*Société des Chemins de Fer Français*), at the main line stations (*gares SNCF*), such as Gare Saint-Lazare, Gare du Nord, Gare Montparnasse, Gare de Lyon, Gare de l'Est etc. In fact there is hardly anwhere in Paris that is more than 500 metres from a *métro* station. Many of the station names are either based on historical events, or associated with important aspects of Paris life.

Cheapness As well as being the quickest form of transport, it is also the cheapest, particularly if you are wise enough to buy a booklet (*carnet*) of tickets, rather than separate tickets for individual journeys. The same ticket can be used whether the journey is long or short, and you can change trains, or change to a different line without paying any more. The same tickets can also be used on buses.

In the rush hours there is a train nearly every 90 seconds, and each carriage has a notice indicating that it can carry twenty passengers seated and 140 standing, yet people are still packed in like sardines!

Recent improvements In recent years the service has been considerably improved, with quieter and smoother trains making travel increasingly comfortable. Thanks to automatic controls, ticket collectors are no longer needed. Lines are being extended and some striking new stations have been built, in an artistic style one hardly associates with stations: for example, Louvre is decorated with reproductions of paintings and works of art, Franklin-Roosevelt has window displays, and you can do some of your shopping at the various brightly decorated shops at Montparnasse and St-Lazare stations.

The *RER (Réseau Express Régional)*

Traffic in Paris
(Photo Clausse – RATP)

Fast links with outer suburbs In addition to the extension and improvement to the ordinary métro services, the construction of a brand-new express *métro* service, the *RER*, with its own lines and stations, is already a magnificent technical achievement: it is now possible to get from one side of Paris to the other in ten minutes. Begun in 1969, with the aim of linking the city centre with some of the outer suburbs by means of a high quality express service, the *RER* is still being extended. In view of the high cost of construction and the quality of the service, it is not surprising that a higher fare is charged on the *RER* than on the ordinary *métro*.

Buses

Paris also has a full bus service which, although slower than the *métro*, has the advantage of allowing the visitor to observe the bustle of Paris life. Buses are usually single-deckers and are painted green and white. Reserved lanes for buses and taxis (there are over 70 km of these) have speeded up the service, and overcome some of the problems created by traffic jams.

Cars and roads

Transport by car is perhaps the least satisfactory means of getting round Paris, for even outside the rush hours one can get stuck in traffic jams and it is difficult (as well as costly) to park. Some of the traffic

Modern transport planning: the road system (with clover leaf) serving Paris Airport at Roissy (Photo Aéroport de Paris – J. J. Moreau)

problems have been reduced by the one-way system and by the new roads or freeways through and round the city centre: the *boulevard périphérique* is an outer ring road 35 km long, begun in 1960 and taking seventeen years to complete; and some of the quays running along the banks of the river have been made into *voies express*, which are fast main roads and help to relieve some of the traffic jams. Many of these join up with the main 'N' roads (*Routes Nationales*) and the motorways or freeways (*autoroutes*) which lead out of the city. Paris is also fortunate in its *grands boulevards* which form an inner ring and an outer ring around Paris, as well as linking across Paris at certain points.

The concern of Parisians for the beauty of the city, with its traditional views and perspectives, has been respected (more than in many cities) by the planners, and wherever possible roads have been built below ground level, so that they should not intrude.

Paris airports

Paris has three airports, linking it to the rest of France and the outside world: Le Bourget (to the north), Orly (to the south) and the ultra-modern new Charles de Gaulle Airport, which was opened in 1974 at Roissy, a few kilometres to the north of Paris.

The Charles de Gaulle Airport cost many millions of francs and was designed not only to replace the older Le Bourget Airport, but was envisaged by General de Gaulle as a major symbol of French prestige. It was lavishly equipped as a kind of space-age project, with moving pavements to convey passengers to 'satellites', (embarkation terminals). It has become one of the busiest airports in Europe despite being plagued by strikes. The airport terminals house luxurious shops and restaurants (but make sure you have plenty of money on you if you decide to have a meal!)

The Paris Charles de Gaulle Airport: showing the central terminal building, with No. 2 Satellite in the foreground (Photo Aéroport de Paris – J. J. Moreau)

The various Paris airports between them handle more air traffic than any other city in Europe, and the Charles de Gaulle Airport alone can handle from eight to ten million passengers a year. The state airline, *Air France*, with its domestic partner *Air Inter*, is one of the largest and busiest airlines in the world.

Modern building in Paris

Although Paris retains most of the old features and land-marks which have been traditionally associated with it, the Paris of today has changed considerably from what it was only a few years ago. The new buildings and new suburbs, the freeways and ring-roads, the hypermarkets, the express *métro* etc., have all helped to add a new dimension to the city.

Among the modern buildings which you can see are:

Le Palais de Chaillot, built before the war, a magnificent complex of buildings in white stone, situated in a most elegant setting on the west side of Paris, looking across the Seine towards the Eiffel Tower beyond.

La Maison de L'UNESCO, (the UNESCO Building), an exciting piece of architecture, built in the shape of a letter 'Y', which is also situated near the Eiffel Tower: it is the centre for many international conferences and exhibitions.

Maine-Montparnasse, on the Left Bank, an adventurous new project on the site of the old Maine-Montparnasse station, which has been extended to redevelop the whole district. At the centre of the development is the great 58-storey tower, which is over 200 m high, and has a helicopter pad on the roof, and a restaurant offering panoramic views over Paris. A new 'U'-shaped station has been built, with eighteen-storey blocks of flats and offices and a multi-level indoor shopping centre. This houses a complete range of shops, from large department stores such as the *Galeries Lafayette* and *C & A* to smaller shops selling books, records, shoes etc. Underneath the shopping centre are car-parks, and a sports centre which includes three swimming pools.

La Défense, an ultra-modern district which has been redeveloped since 1958 on the site of a former slum area on the west side of Paris. Instead of knocking down a few buildings at a time and putting up a new building here and there, the planner re-thought and re-planned the area as a whole. The slums were entirely demolished and in their place a brand-new miniature town was planned and built, not just as a collection of buildings, but as a basis for a complete community, with blocks of flats, offices, shops, banks, cinemas and restaurants, as well as the University of Paris 10. It is anticipated that eventually 100 000

What life is like at ground level at La Défense

Modern building developments at La Défense – *looking towards the centre of Paris (Photo EPAD)*

people will be working in the offices and shops, and that the flats will offer accommodation for 20 000 people.

A ring-road round the town, and a motorway underneath the town provide fast and efficient transport, and the whole complex is linked by the express *métro* (*RER*) to the centre of Paris.

Le Centre National des Industries et Techniques (CNIT) is the French National Centre for Industry and Technology, one of the most striking buildings in the development at *La Défense*. Built in the shape of a shell, it houses a conference centre and an exhibition hall.

Les Halles, the former site of the wholesale fruit and vegetable market, has recently undergone a major redevelopment. The removal of the market to its new purpose-built accommodation outside Paris at Rungis has provided planners with a challenge: how best to take advantage of the huge gap left in the middle of the city.

After much controversy and argument, plans were eventually drawn up for five levels of buildings, going down 16 m for the new Express *métro* station. This has meant digging a great hole (the famous *grand trou*) in the city centre which now accommodates a new shopping and leisure centre known as the *Forum des Halles*. *Level 3* provides accommodation for recreation (restaurants, cafés, cinema, bookshops and car parks, and later a library, swimming pool, skating rink and gymnasium); *Level 2* is mainly for motorists and taxis, but also contains a market for shoppers; *Level 1* consists of open-air gardens, and on *Level Zéro*, which is ground level, are gardens and an art gallery. Provision has been made for a children's play area of 4180 square metres. This remarkable development was formally opened in September 1979.

Le Centre Georges Pompidou. One of the most dramatic buildings forming part of the redevelopment of *Les Halles* is the new Pompidou Centre, designed by a team of one English and two Italian architects. Constructed largely of glass, it is unusual in the way that lifts and staircases have been built on the outside of the building, so as to create the maximum space within. It contains a museum and art gallery, housing the National Collection of Contemporary Art, as well as facilities for exhibitions, lectures, film shows etc.

Le Centre National et de Culture Georges Pompidou
(Photo Jean-Philippe Reverdot)

Development and town planning in Paris

In order to reduce the concentration of industry and population in Paris, the government produced a vast plan for the future development of the city, as part of an overall national plan, which included the development of the Regions (see Section D: The Provinces and Regions of France). Firms were discouraged from either setting up or extending their work in Paris; new towns and suburbs were built outside Paris; companies and organisations were transferred out of the city centre; new roads and motorways were constructed to relieve the traffic congestion; and the *métro* itself was extended and improved. Because more and more people have been moving further out of Paris, the town centre, other than in the entertainment areas, has become increasingly deserted at night. (It also means that the average Paris worker spends between two or three hours a day travelling to and from work: so it is clear that Paris is very much a city of commuters.)

New towns

As part of the plan for the future development of Paris, a decision was made in 1966 to plan and build five completely new towns, between ten and 35 km outside Paris in the country: at Cergy-Pontoise, Evry, Marne-la-Vallée, Melun-Sénart and St Quentin-en-Yvelines.

These were a tremendous feat of planning as well as building, for they were conceived as complete towns, providing facilities for work, shopping and recreation for communities of between 100 000 and 200 000 people.

The lay-out of the new town of Cergy-Pontoise (Photo Interphototheque – DF)

Evry

An example of the sort of thing that happened was in the new town of Evry, which now stands on acres and acres of former farm-land. Teams of planners, architects and engineers descended on the site,

The new town of Evry, at ground level
(Photo D. Planquette – E.P.A.V.E.)

and shortly afterwards set about the task of creating a complete town out of nothing. The result is a splendid modern town and community, complete with council offices, schools, commercial buildings and law courts, surrounded by gardens. A brand-new shopping centre has been built in traditional style, with individual shops. So that people can relax and enjoy themselves as well as work in the new town, there are cinemas, a skating rink, cafés, a theatre with seats for 600 people, a swimming-pool and a large library. To ensure that people can get to and from the town centre, four bus services link it with the outskirts, and a motorway provides a rapid link with Paris.

At present 12 000 people live in Evry, but within ten years the number is expected to rise to 400 000. These are the people who will be able to decide how successful the planners have been.

Other new towns

In addition there are new developments at Créteil and Parly, similar to those at *La Défense*. They contain new regional commercial centres, with a wide range of facilities, such as shops, cafés, cinemas, car parks etc. These attract large numbers of customers from far afield: many of them live considerable distances from Paris, and prefer not to travel into Paris to do their shopping.

These new centres reflect the changes in modern social and business life in France. Until around 1960 French shops had kept their traditional character, based on the small local shopkeeper; but the spread of suburbs further and further from the town centres resulted in changes. With the increase in the use of deep-freezers, and with more people owning cars, more and more housewives found it convenient to shop once a week, buying larger quantities at places where they could park their cars close enough to load up all their shopping.

SECTION D: THE PROVINCES AND REGIONS OF FRANCE

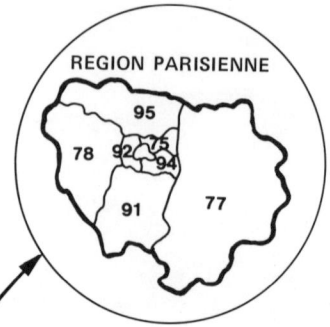

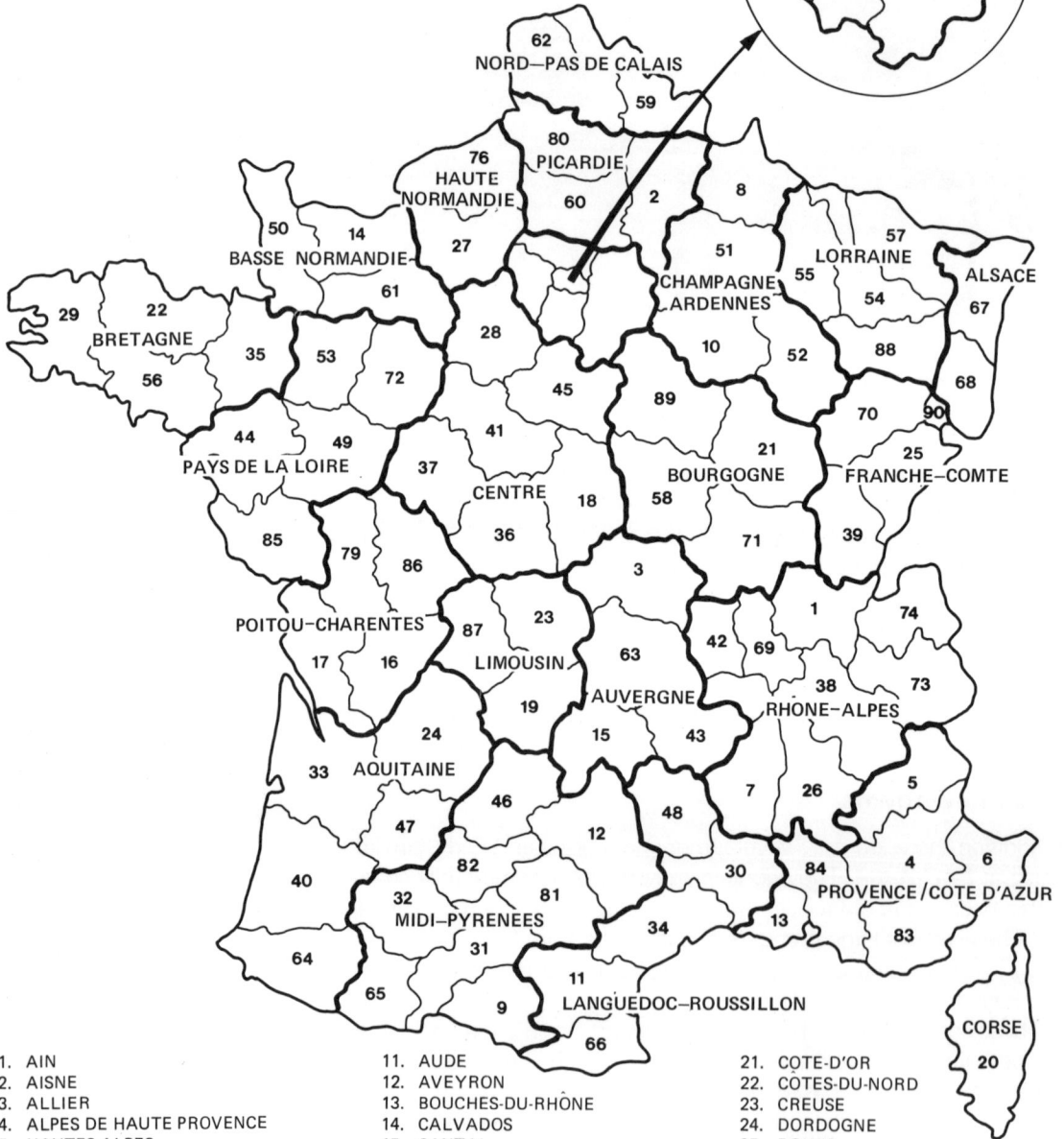

REGION PARISIENNE

95
78 92 75 94
91 77

NORD—PAS DE CALAIS
62
59

PICARDIE
80
76 HAUTE NORMANDIE 60 2 8

BASSE NORMANDIE
50 14 27
61 28

CHAMPAGNE ARDENNES
51 55 LORRAINE 57 ALSACE
10 54 67
52 88 68
89 70 90

BRETAGNE
29 22
35 53 72 45
56

PAYS DE LA LOIRE
44 49
37 41
85 79 86 CENTRE 36 18 58 BOURGOGNE 21 FRANCHE—COMTE 25
71 39

POITOU-CHARENTES
17 16 87 23 LIMOUSIN 63 42 69 1 74
19 AUVERGNE 38 73
24 15 43 RHONE—ALPES
33 AQUITAINE 46 7 26 5
47 12 48
40 82 30 84 4 6
32 81 PROVENCE/COTE D'AZUR
64 MIDI-PYRENEES 34 13 83
31
65 11 LANGUEDOC—ROUSSILLON
9 66 CORSE
20

1. AIN	11. AUDE	21. COTE-D'OR
2. AISNE	12. AVEYRON	22. COTES-DU-NORD
3. ALLIER	13. BOUCHES-DU-RHONE	23. CREUSE
4. ALPES DE HAUTE PROVENCE	14. CALVADOS	24. DORDOGNE
5. HAUTES ALPES	15. CANTAL	25. DOUBS
6. ALPES MARITIMES	16. CHARENTE	26. DROME
7. ARDECHE	17. CHARENTE-MARITIME	27. EURE
8. ARDENNES	18. CHER	28. EURE-ET-LOIR
9. ARIEGE	19. CORREZE	29. FINISTERE
10. AUBE	20. CORSE	30. GARD

Origins

The 95 départements

Provinces Although France has been one country for many centuries, the ancient provinces and regions have kept their own individual character, customs and even language. Even today many French people consider themselves to be first and foremost Bretons, Basques, Auvergnats, etc. There were originally 30 historic provinces and many of them were at one time largely independent, or even separate kingdoms. It was mainly because of this that the French kings tried to bring them under the central control of Paris.

Napoleon also wanted to increase the control of Paris, and he decided to split up the 30 provinces into 90 *départements*, each under the control of a *préfet*, who was responsible only to Paris. It is this system which still exists in France: each *département* is numbered (see map p. 68) and these numbers are shown today in the postal codes and in car number plates (so you can tell at a glance which *département* a car has come from.)

Independence In spite of the efforts of the French kings, Napoleon and more recent presidents, however, this desire for greater independence has increased rather than decreased in the last few years. In fact there are active independence movements among the Bretons and the Basques, who want to cut themselves off altogether from the rest of France; and many of these have given rise to demonstrations and often violent confrontations with the police.

It is tempting to think of France as consisting of two parts; Paris and the rest of the country. The rest of France, i.e. provincial France, has been spoken of as the 'French desert', because so much of its life was drained away to Paris: people, jobs, money, cultural activities, etc. The result has been a concentration of population and economic as well as cultural strength in Paris, which has created an imbalance between Paris and the rest of France.

The effects of this imbalance were:
1. too many activities concentrated in a small area;
2. too heavy a load on the resources of Paris, which has led to congestion;
3. an uneven spread of population and talent, i.e. too much in Paris and too little elsewhere;
4. the rest of France has been drained of its economic strength (particular examples of this are the Massif Central and the south-west). This has led to a shortage of jobs, which in turn has caused many young people to leave their home areas to seek work in the cities.

This movement, known as the 'rural exodus', or flight from the countryside, can be measured by the fact that before the war 35 per cent of the population lived in the country, but now the proportion has dropped to fifteen per cent, and over half of these are over 55 years of age. (Within a period of fifteen years, five million jobs in agriculture disappeared, and over half a million in mining.)

An elderly farmer cultivating his crops in the traditional way (Photo YAN – DF)

Depopulation As a result, Paris has been crowded with more people than it could cope with, whilst at the same time countless country villages have lost the majority of their population, leaving deserted and often derelict houses and cottages. Some of these are now being bought up as second homes or holiday cottages, which are more common in France than in most countries in Europe, and where people use them not only for holidays but as weekend retreats from the pressures of town life. Many people who work in the towns still hanker after the country life which they or their families gave up not so long ago for the attractions of better paid jobs, the 'bright lights' and apparently 'easier' life of the cities.

The development of the regions: French regional policy

The increasing awareness of these problems, and of the need to get a better balance between Paris and the regions, led in the early 1950s to the French policy for regional development. The purpose of this was:
1. to try to strengthen the regions outside Paris;
2. by creating more jobs and industrial development, to encourage young people to stay, and older people to return to live and work in their home areas.

Solutions In order to deal with these problems, new plans were proposed:
1. *Métropoles* In order to reduce the concentration on Paris, it was decided to expand eight towns (or combinations of neighbouring towns), which were to be made into eight new metropolitan centres called *métropoles d'équilibre*. These are shown on the map at the top of p. 71.
2. *Regions* In 1965 it was decided to group the 90 former *départements* into 22 new regions (i.e. 21 plus Corsica).

The new regions, whilst not replacing the *départements*, which continued to exist and retained all their rights, were basically intended to produce larger economic units, under the control of new super-prefects, who were responsible for the coordination of the economic planning and development of their regions. At the same time the central government, by various financial incentives, encouraged firms to expand in the regions rather than in Paris. In 1973 the government took its policy a stage further by setting up a regional council and an economic and social planning committee, each with the power to make decisions. Major schemes for the development of tourism were devised, and among those areas to benefit from them were the Languedoc-Roussillon coast, (the *côte vermeille*), where six new resorts were to be built, the Aquitaine coast, and Corsica.

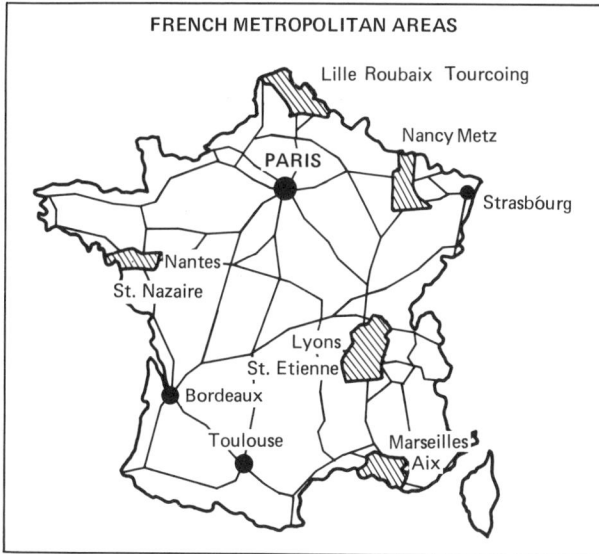

FRENCH METROPOLITAN AREAS

In 1981 the new government of President Mitterrand introduced important measures in his policy of *decentralisation* to cut back the traditional power of the central government in Paris, by reducing the power of the government-appointed Prefects who had often vetoed decisions made by representative assemblies in the *départments* and regions.

Right, the Maison de la Culture *of the 20th arrondissement in Paris (Photo H. Guirard)*

Results The success of these plans can be judged from two facts:
1. Since 1975, for the first time for centuries, more people have been moving from Paris to the regions than the other way round.
2. The new urban centres (*métropoles*) have attracted so much of the life of their region that since 1973 the government has left them to develop on their own. It has therefore tried to encourage the growth of the smaller towns which were in danger of being overshadowed within their regions by the *métropoles*. As well as encouraging the economic growth of the towns it has tried to stimulate cultural life by setting up *Maisons de la Culture* which are well-equipped arts and leisure centres for activities such as concerts, films, meetings, recreation etc. These have represented a striking development in the life of certain provincial towns, which have benefited from the whole range of cultural activities: they have helped to dispel the traditional image of the French provincial town as a cultural 'backwater', and in particular to make the younger generation feel that they do not have to migrate to Paris in order to enjoy these sorts of activities.

The effect of these new measures was that, despite the fact that from 1968–75 over 200 000 foreign workers came to live in Paris, more than 110 000 more French people actually left Paris than arrived.

The northern industrial area: Nord/Pas-de-Calais

This area, which skirts the Belgian border, includes the *départements* of **Nord** and **Pas-de-Calais**, together with the ancient provinces of Picardy, Artois and Flanders. It is the largest industrial and coal-mining area in France. Like most industrial areas it is characterised by mills, factories etc., and criss-crossed by roads and canals. Yet in spite of all the factories, the towns manage to remain remarkably clean.

Battle-grounds It is a region remembered as the scene of many of the bloodiest battles in history: the Somme and Arras (during World War I), where literally hundreds of thousands of men were killed or injured. In World War II, the beaches of Dunkirk were made famous in 1940 by the evacuation in an armada of small craft of British and other troops, who were surrounded by the Germans.

Many of the towns were largely destroyed during the battles, and as a result much of the building is new, though some of the towns still bear the traces of war; you can visit the huge cemeteries of war graves, and on the beaches some of the German fortifications still remain.

Incidentally the Armistice Day poppies represent the poppies that covered the fields of Flanders, which allied soldiers associated with the scenes of the battles where they lost so many of their friends.

Industry

The two main areas of industry are:
1. *Lille* – which has combined with Roubaix and Tourcoing to form one of the new *métropoles*, or urban development centres. The traditional industry here is textiles: wool, flax and cotton. Nowadays man-made textiles and carpets are increasingly taking over from the traditional textiles.
2. *The Coalfield* – based on small towns like Lens and Douai, produces 55 per cent of France's total coal production. Here the industries are coal and steel (and associated industries such as tubes, wire, machinery and boilers, etc.) Unfortunately, the spread of new methods in the coal and steel industries has led to increasing unemployment, as men have been replaced by machines in the more mechanical jobs.

Ports

The main port of the area is Dunkirk (**Dunkerque**), now France's third busiest port. Other ports are Boulogne, France's leading fishing port, which with Calais and Dunkirk serves the cross-Channel traffic.

Population

This area houses nearly four million people (or about eight per cent of the whole of the population of France). Many of the miners and other industrial workers are foreign workers, who come from places like North Africa, Italy, Portugal, Poland, etc.

Although most of the work in the area is based on industry, other forms of work exist, and provide much-needed variety in the type of jobs available.

Agriculture

Although only about ten per cent of the people work in agriculture, the area produces about one fifth of all French sugar beet, as well as potatoes, pork and wheat (particularly in Flanders). Wine, including the famous *Champagne*, is produced in the area from which it takes its name.

The Chambre de Commerce *at Lille*
(Photo J. Feuillie)

Tourism

Many tourists come to the sea-side resorts, of which the elegant and fashionable **Le Touquet** is one of the most famous, with its casino, night-clubs, yachting etc. They are also attracted to famous cathedrals like **Reims**, which rivals Chartres in its beauty, and **Amiens**.

The Ile de France and the Paris region

In spite of its name, the **Ile de France** is not an island at all, but is the area formed by the Seine and its tributaries, and is the historic centre of France, just as Paris is its historic capital. Although the Ile de France is nowadays dominated by Paris and its satellite towns and industrial developments, the land here is lush and green, with valleys and forests, including ancient royal hunting forests, and many reminders of France's history in the form of churches, cathedrals and castles (or *châteaux*).

Cathedrals The cathedral at **Beauvais** is reputed to be the tallest in the world. **Chartres** cathedral is one of the finest in Europe, and is particularly famous for its medieval stained glass.

Châteaux In addition, a number of imposing *châteaux* are associated with many of the great men and events in France's history. Some of the most famous are:

Saint-Germain-en-Laye, built by François I, it was, until 1682, the residence of Louis XI;

Rambouillet, today the summer residence of the President of the Republic;

Fontainebleau, built by François I and set within the former royal hunting forest, it was one of the favourite residences of Napoleon I;

Versailles, perhaps the best known of all, built by Louis XIV as the centre of his court, and one of his great achievements. Louis began building Versailles at the age of 23, and the work continued for 50 years. This enormous palace, together with its 100 hectares of formal gardens, ornamental lakes and fountains, is not only one of the most impressive buildings in Europe, but more than almost any other symbolises an age and the king who dominated it. It also set a fashion which was copied not only in France, but in many other countries, including Britain, where many stately homes were influenced by the grandiose style of Versailles.

The Palace of Versailles

Normandy

Historical origins

Normandy, like most of France, was occupied by the Romans; after the Romans came the Vikings and Norsemen, from whom its name is derived.

William the Conqueror Normandy developed into an independent dukedom and in 1066 Duke William of Normandy led his army in an armada of ships across the Channel to invade England. He landed near Hastings where he fought and defeated Harold, the king of England, at the Battle of Hastings.

Links with England William was crowned king, and then began the long Norman occupation of England. One of the effects of this, apart from introducing Norman and French customs, architecture and language to England, was to unite Normandy with the crown of England. It remained a part of England until 1204 when it was regained by France, only to be won back by England during the Hundred Years War. By 1450 the French finally gained control of Normandy, leaving only the Channel Islands as the sole reminder of their former Norman territory. This is why the Channel Islands seem so very French to most English-speaking people who visit them today.

World War II Many years later, during World War II, Normandy was the scene of the allied landings in 1944, which led to the liberation of France and of Europe. Many reminders of the war are still to be seen, including concrete block-houses and gun-emplacements. These formed part of the so-called Atlantic Wall, which was not a wall at all, but a series of fortifications built by the Germans along the Atlantic and Channel coasts as a defence against the allied invasions.

Modern dairy farming in Normandy (P. Bringe – Photo Ministère de l'Agriculture)

Situation

For many of us Normandy is the first place we see when we go to France, for it lies just across the Channel from Britain; it is under two hours by rail from the Normandy coast to Paris.

Its position on the north-west coast of France enables it to benefit from the Gulf Stream, which causes the mild, damp climate that produces the lush countryside so suitable for its farming.

Farming

This is largely flat, rich land, with orchards of cider apples. It is also famous for dairy farming, producing milk, butter and cheese. (*Camembert* and *Pont l'Evêque* are two famous cheeses of the area.)

Mont Saint-Michel (Photo J. Feuillie)

Tourism

On the coast are several popular holiday resorts, including **Mont Saint-Michel**, **Trouville**, **Dieppe**, **Honfleur** and the fashionable **Deauville**. The fine medieval monastery at Mont Saint-Michel is situated on the top of a rock on the tiny island of that name. In order to reach it, you have to climb over 900 steps. At certain times of the year the sands between the island and the mainland are exposed, but there are dangerous quicksands, and the tide comes racing in at over 60 m a minute, or over 1 m a second … so it is no place for dawdling!

Traditional houses – and occupations: Honfleur, Calvados (Photo French Government Tourist Office)

Tourists are also attracted to the cathedrals of Rouen, Bayeux and Evreux, and to abbeys such as that at **Caen**, which is a university town as well as the regional capital.

Ports

Normandy's position on the coast has resulted in a number of busy ports: **Dieppe** (cross-channel trade), **Cherbourg**, the river-port of **Rouen** (France's fourth largest port), and **Le Havre**, which is not only France's second port (after Marseilles), but thanks to the construction of the massive new oil terminal at **Antifer**, ranks as the third oil port in Europe, and is equipped to receive the new half-million tonne supertankers.

Petrol tanker entering the port of Le Havre (Photo Port autonome du Havre)

Industry

Although traditionally this has always been a rural farming area, considerable industrial expansion is taking place in the so-called Lower Seine Complex at Le Havre, which has oil refineries with direct links to Paris. Just inland in the same area is the ancient town of **Rouen**, with its historic associations with Joan of Arc, who was burned to death in 1431 by the English.

Brittany

Traditions

Brittany is the beautiful and largely undeveloped home of a very independent people, the Bretons, whose native language, Breton, is still spoken by over a million people in many parts, particularly the west, and forms the basis of their own literature and newspapers. The Bretons have such a strong sense of independence that for some time they have been conducting an active campaign to be separated from the rest of France. The separatist movement has been responsible for a number of demonstrations: roads have been blocked by tractors, the entrance to town halls blocked with farm produce, etc. The Bretons have many historical and cultural links with their Celtic cousins in Cornwall, Wales and Ireland, and were not part of France until 1532.

Pardons

Brittany has strong religious traditions, reflected in its churches and calvaries The *Pardons* are religious celebrations at which people either take vows or ask for forgiveness. These celebrations include long, slow, processions of people dressed in traditional costumes (not unlike those of the Welsh, with lace head-dresses for the women), carrying banners and statues shoulder-high. The *Pardons* are widespread throughout Brittany, and most small towns and villages have their own. After the completion of the religious part of the celebration, the whole population takes part in general festivities, including music and dancing.

Problems

Brittany is a classic example of the problems which French government planning has tried to solve. Whereas Paris has offered too many attractions in the form of jobs, Brittany (along with a number of other regions) has suffered from having too many people and not enough jobs. As a result, many people have left Brittany and gone elsewhere, mainly to Paris: the population dropped by over one third in the fifteen years after World War II.

Atlantic

Brittany is situated on a peninsula jutting out into the Atlantic Ocean, and it is the Atlantic which is the greatest influence on the countryside: it brings fresh winds, rain to keep the fields and pastures green and lush and the warmth of the Gulf Stream, which gives the area such a mild climate.

It is the Atlantic, therefore, which is largely responsible for Brittany's three main activities: farming, fishing and tourism.

Farming

Farming is traditionally the main occupation in Brittany. One tenth of all French milk comes from Brittany and much of this is converted into butter and cheese. As well as being the main poultry-producing area of France, Brittany grows potatoes and early vegetables (cauliflowers, peas and artichokes).

Fishing

Along the coast, the traditional occupation is fishing, largely in the Bay of Biscay. The principal fishing ports are **Lorient**, **Concarneau**, **Douarnenez** and **Saint-Malo**.

Ports

Nantes (a town of a quarter of a million people) and **Saint-Nazaire** are busy commercial ports, whilst **Brest** and **Lorient** are bases for the French navy.

Industry

Some industrial expansion has taken place in the region, particularly round the mouth of the Loire, based on **Nantes** and **Rennes**, the former provincial capital. An exciting tidal power station was built in 1967 on the River Rance (near Dinard and Saint-Malo), where the power of the tides has been harnessed to provide electricity. (The advantages of situating the project here are that the rise and fall of the tides in the Rance estuary are among the highest in France; and also that there are four tides in 24 hours compared with the usual two.) You can visit the huge electricity generating plant which now dominates the mouth of the river.

In a period when everyone is concerned about the limited supply of oil and the possible dangers of nuclear energy, this is one of the most advanced projects of its type in the world, and involved blocking the

A Breton fishing post: Plovezet, Port d'Audierne in Finistère (Photo Jahan – DF)

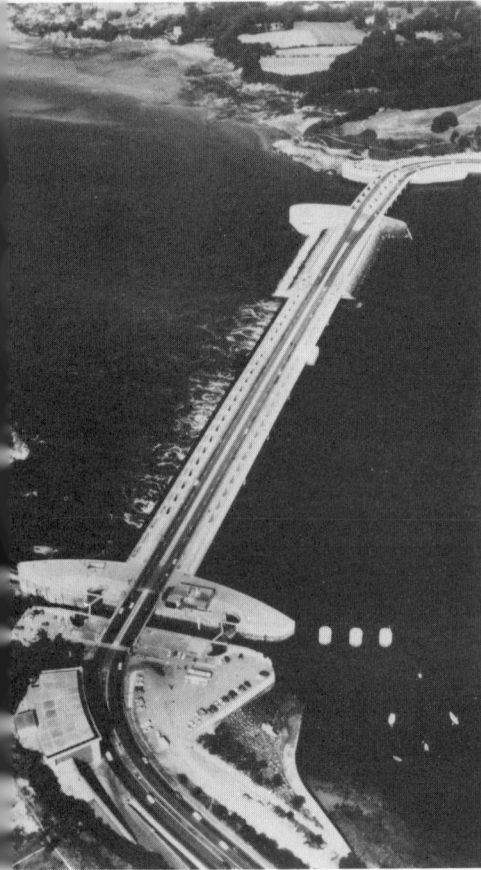

Above, aerial view of the tidal power station on the Rance (Photo M. Brigaud, Sodel DF)

Right, Nantes, the capital and main town of the area (Photo B. Beaujard – DF)

River Rance by the construction of a huge dam. One of its greatest advantages is that the tides, which are the source of the power, are both free of charge and can never be exhausted.

Tourism

Tourism has become increasingly significant in Brittany, and a number of flourishing sea-side resorts can be found along the 1200 km of coast-line, including the elegant **Dinard** and **La Baule** (complete with casino, cafés, restaurants and discothèques), and fishing ports such as **Saint-Malo**.

As well as these larger resorts, many pretty little fishing villages are dotted amongst the coves and inlets along the coast. Among other smaller resorts are **Concarneau** and **Carnac** (where about 3000 prehistoric monuments have been found.)

Western France and the Atlantic coast: Poitou-Charentes

This is a long stretch of land along the coast of the Atlantic which extends from the Loire in the north to the Gironde in the south.

The climate of the whole area is mild and warm due to the effects of the Atlantic.

Vendée

The northern part of this region, known as the Vendée, has long sandy beaches, backed by dunes and pine trees. The country inland is generally flat and low-lying, with fields, hedges and some marshes, as well as a series of fresh-water lakes covering about 80 000 hectares. The French government has launched a big campaign to develop the tourist industry in the area, as part of recent plans to develop new industries in under-developed areas.

Poitou-Charentes

This is the southern part of the region, which includes some sandy coast line, but also many ancient villages and historic towns, surrounded by peaceful vineyards. Inland where the land is not cultivated, heaths and forests predominate.

On the coast is the fishing port and yachting centre of **La Rochelle**. The ultra-modern resort of **Royan**, which was completely destroyed in 1945, has been rebuilt with brilliantly imaginative modern buildings, and facilities for over 2000 yachts.

The beach at Royan, Charentes: note the modern building in the background (Photo J. Feuillie)

Produce

Wine This is a major wine-growing area, and perhaps the best-known product of the vineyards of the region is *cognac*.

Dairy There is also a good deal of dairy-farming in the area, where cattle are reared, and some of the best butter in France is produced.

Fishing The ancient town of La Rochelle is the busiest fishing port on the Atlantic coast, as well as a tourist attraction in its own right.

The university town of **Poitiers** and the port of **La Rochelle** are the largest towns in the area.

Alsace — Lorraine — Les Vosges

This is in the north-eastern corner of France, parts of which skirt the borders of Belgium to the north, and stretch as far as the Rhine and the German frontier to the east. It is a region which, though it often looks more like Germany than France, and even the local dialect sounds more like German than French, remains essentially French in the feelings of its people.

Alsace and Lorraine have more than once changed hands between France and Germany, and have been the scene of much fighting between the two countries, during the 1870 Franco-Prussian War, and the two World Wars. One of the most bitter battles of World War I was fought at **Verdun**, where enormous numbers of men were killed on both sides.

Alsace

Alsace is part of the Rhine Valley, and is a centre for the production of potash. The major town and capital of the area is **Strasbourg**, which has a magnificent Gothic cathedral. Strasbourg is important for oil-refining, engineering and chemical industries, as well as being a busy inland port, linked to the Rhine and the Marne-Rhine canal. A town of over 200 000 inhabitants, it has gained further importance as the home of the Council of Europe and the European Parliament.

Lorraine

Lorraine lies to the west of the region, irrigated by the Meuse and the Moselle (famous for the wine produced in its valley). This is an important industrial area, important for its iron and steel industries (90 per cent of France's iron ore is mined here), as well as for coal mining. Lorraine is also a centre for the production of glass, textiles and electrical goods. The main towns in Lorraine are **Nancy**, the elegant capital city, and **Metz**.

Strasbourg capital of Alsace, and seat of the European Parliament (Photo M. Brigaud — Sodel DF)

Les Vosges

This is a highland area separating Lorraine from Alsace, and much of the land is moorland or forests, which supply the paper mills. It is also the home of the French cotton industry, the main centres of which are **Mulhouse** and **Colmar**.

Agriculture

Although this is a major industrial region of France, much of the land is devoted to agriculture. The main crops, apart from the grapes, are cereals, sugar beet and potatoes, as well as hops for beer, and vines which produce the Moselle and Riesling wines.

Nancy, The Place Stanislas and the hôtel de ville, floodlit

Burgundy, the Jura and the Franche-Comté

Burgundy

Burgundy is part of the heartland of France, and its ancient capital of **Dijon** was a route-centre for people travelling between the north and south. Famous for its vineyards and the wonderful wines they produce, it is at the heart of what is often called the 'eating and drinking country'. Among the lush, wooded hills and valleys are many interesting old towns and villages.

The Jura

Based on the former province of Franche-Comté, this is an area of mountains and forests, close to the border with Switzerland. The mountains form a natural barrier 240 kilometres long and between 40 and 80 kilometres wide, and attract many tourists. The forests provide the timber which is the raw material of some of the main wood-based industries, such as furniture, toys etc. This is also where the famous *Gruyère* cheese is made.

The largest town of the area is **Besançon**, which is a university town, as well as a centre for the manufacture of plastics, cheese and the apéritif, *Pernod*.

Besançon: the ramparts
(Photo B. Rouget)

The Loire Valley : Anjou and Touraine

This is one of the most beautiful and fascinating regions of France, and is dominated by the Loire, which is the longest of all French rivers (1000 km). The countryside is lush and green, with wooded valleys, and the climate is warm and mild: this combination enables a rich variety of fruit and flowers to be grown in the region, which fully deserves its title as the 'Garden of France'.

Anjou and Touraine

These are two of France's ancient provinces, rich in historical associations and many visible reminders of France's past, in particular the *châteaux*. There are some 120 of these magnificent buildings, and they vary from medieval fortresses to royal palaces and stately homes. It is difficult to imagine any area of equal size with so many buildings of such interest and beauty, set in such beautiful countryside. The interest and splendour of the *châteaux* are often heightened by the *son et lumière* shows, which dramatise their history by the clever use of lighting and music, etc. Some of the finest *châteaux* are at **Amboise**, **Chenonceaux**, **Blois**, **Chambord** and **Azay-le-Rideau**.

Tourism

Many thousands of tourists flock here every year from all over the world, attracted by the *châteaux*, cathedrals such as those at **Bourges** and **Tours**, the warm gentle climate, the fascinating old towns and villages and the beauty of the countryside. They also find excellent facilities for camping on the many camp-sites, whilst the rivers provide opportunities for swimming.

Towns

The area has no really large industrial towns; the largest towns are **Tours**, **Orléans**, **Bourges**, **Angers** and **Le Mans** (famous for its 24-hour motor race).

*The Château de Chambord
(Photo French Government Tourist Office)*

South-west France and Aquitaine: the Dordogne, Les Landes, the Pyrenees and the Basque country

Characteristics

The south-west region of France forms a triangle of low land between the Atlantic to the west, the Pyrenees and the Spanish frontier to the south and the Massif Central to the north-east. The main characteristics of the area are: mountains (Pyrenees and Massif Central); coastlands (along the Atlantic); and lowlands (Les Landes and Gascony).

Weather

The weather is generally dry, with mild winters and hot summers, yet the land does not suffer from lack of rain, as plenty of water is brought down by the rivers from the surrounding mountains. The result is that the land is well watered and much richer than might be expected from the climate.

Bordeaux and the Gironde

Rócamadour (Photo P. J. Downes)

This is above all a wine-producing area: vines are grown almost everywhere in the region. **Bordeaux**, which once belonged to England, is the largest town of the area (with a population of a quarter of a million), and is famous not only as the centre of the wine trade, but gives its name to an important type of wine. Other famous wines produced in the area are *graves* and *sauternes*, much of which are exported. Large quantities of ordinary table wines (*vin ordinaire*) are produced, mainly to be bought and drunk in France.

The Dordogne/Périgord

The Périgord lies inland to the east of Bordeaux, and is more commonly known to tourists as the **Dordogne** area, after the name of the picturesque River Dordogne, which flows through the region. It is an area of great natural beauty, which has been virtually untouched for centuries. Recently, however, it has been discovered by many thousands of tourists, and has now developed (largely since the end of World War II) into a major tourist area. People come from all over the world to enjoy the scenery with its quiet rivers, which are ideal for swimming, and its rich green valleys.

Among the many places of historical interest are the **Lascaux Caves**, with their prehistoric wall paintings. These caves were discovered in 1940 when four young men were searching for a dog which had disappeared down a hole. When they went down after it they found a series of caves with walls covered in magnificent paintings, over 20 000 years old, and showing the animals that men hunted in those days: bulls, bison and deer. The colours — browns, greys and black — are still perfectly preserved today, though the caves have had to be closed to the public, to prevent the effects of damage from the light and the condensation of people's breath.

Other attractions are the ancient *châteaux*, and the medieval towns of **Sarlat**, **Angoulême**, **Périgueux**, **Cahors** and **Pau**.

Lourdes

Situated not far from Pau, Lourdes is a centre for pilgrims, especially the rich who come (on crutches and in wheelchairs) from all over the world to seek the miracle of a cure. Over two million visitors come to Lourdes every year, drawn by their faith in the story of a fourteen-year-old girl, Bernadette Soubirous, the daughter of a poor miller of Lourdes. In 1858 she claimed that she had seen a vision of the Virgin Mary near the Grotto of Massabielle. After a series of further visions, water miraculously appeared in a spring which had not previously been

Lourdes (Photo YAN)

known. Out of the belief in this miracle grew the faith which has inspired so many pilgrims. Unfortunately the number of visitors has meant that the old town is over-run with tourist shops and other 'attractions'.

Les Landes

This is an unspoiled area of 4800 square kilometres of pine forests, rivers and lakes. Many people come for the fishing and watersports, as well as to enjoy the unique atmosphere of an area which is largely untouched by the effects of modern industrial 'civilisation'. The pine forests, which are one of the characteristics of the area, were originally planted to prevent sand drifting inland from the dunes along the coast. They now provide timber, partly for export and partly for the local paper-making industry.

The coast and forest of Les Landes *(Photo left, A. Perceval – DF; right Photo Janine Nièpce)*

The Pyrenees and the Basque country

This part of the Pyrenees is known as the *Pyrénées Atlantiques*, as it is the part closest to the Atlantic. Among the many holiday resorts along the coast, the largest is **Biarritz**, which is one of France's most famous resorts. Some of the best surfing beaches in Europe are along this coast.

The Basques are an ancient race who live on both sides of the Pyrenees. Their language and culture (and even their origins) are different from those of the people of both France and Spain. Their language is not just an accent or a dialect of French or Spanish, but is quite different from either. They have their own customs, dances and entertainments, and also their own costume, which includes a beret (for the men), rope-soled shoes called *espadrilles*, and a stick which at one time acted as both weapon and walking-stick. The national sport of the Basques is *pelote*, a game in which the players wear a kind of basket strapped to their right arm with which to sling a ball against a wall.

Agriculture

The main activity in the area is traditionally the production of wines, which are mostly the cheaper table wines. The river valleys and the hill slopes of the **Garonne** and the **Dordogne** provide good conditions for market-gardening and fruit growing (plums, peaches, apples and pears).

Industry

Further developments in recent times have been the increasing spread and importance of tourism the discovery of natural gas at **Lacq** (not far from Biarritz), and of oil at **Parentis**. The gas and oil, although not enough for France's needs, have been particularly welcome at a time of high prices for energy.

Basques playing their national sport, Pelote

Languedoc–Roussillon and the Midi-Pyrenees

Languedoc

This is a sun-drenched region stretching for 180 km along the western end of the Mediterranean from the Pyrenees and the Spanish border in the west to the broad river Rhône near Marseilles on the coast. The Languedoc is the area in which traditionally the *langue d'oc* is spoken, i.e. the language of Southern France, where the word *oc* is used for *oui*. This language is spoken (usually as an addition to French) by some ten million people.

It is an area of great character and great variety. The countryside varies from the spectacular peaks of the Eastern Pyrenees to the hot beaches of the Mediterranean. In the plains between, much of the land is devoted to vine-growing, and more wine is produced in this area than anywhere else in France, though most of it is table wine and not for export. Among the famous wines produced are *banyuls* and *rivesaltes*, named after the small towns where they are produced.

Catalans

The western part, near the Spanish border and dominated by the Pyrenees and the ancient city of **Perpignan** (the ancient capital of the kings of Majorca), shows a strong Spanish influence. This can be felt everywhere, not only in the way of life but even in the appearance of the people, with their black hair and dark complexions. This is the centre of the French Catalans, who, like the Bretons and Basques, see themselves as an independent people within France, though the majority of Catalans live in Spain where there is a strong movement for independence. They have their own traditions, culture and language, and these are reflected in their own newspaper. Their fascinating native dance is the *sardane*, which is not just a kind of old-fashioned folk dance, but is still popular and danced by many of the population on *jours de fête*.

Camargue

In the east the Camargue, which is often referred to as France's 'cowboy country', is an area of rolling plains and marshes, where wild horses have been tended and rounded up by horsemen whose work resembles in many ways that of the cowboys of the 'Wild West'. Part of their job is to rear bulls for the local sport of bull-fighting. However, this traditional picture of the Camargue is nowadays being added to, if not changed, by the intensive growing of rice. In addition **Aigues-Mortes** is now the centre of a major new development in the wine industry; new mechanised methods of wine production, based on

The Camargue

new projects in California, are introducing the advantages of mass production to the French wine industry. The grapes are gathered by machines, instead of by hand, and large quantities of wine are made by a series of automatic processes. Eventually the wine emerges into great tanks, rather like petrol storage tanks — all very different from the traditional picture of wine-making in France!

Industry

This is an area which is in the process of great new developments. **Toulouse** is a medieval university town where new industries were developed during World War I. More recently modern industries (including electronics) have been established and Toulouse is now one of the most important centres of the French aero-space industry: it was here that the French part of Concorde was developed.

Montpellier is another ancient university town which is also developing a range of modern industries.

Tourism

The traditional tourist attractions here are the impressive mountain scenery of the Pyrenees to the west; the **Cévennes**, and the spectacular valley and **Gorges du Tarn** to the north; and the wild, untamed country of the **Camargue** to the east. Among the many fascinating places of interest are: the unique medieval walled city of **Carcassonne**, the Roman towns of **Nîmes** (with its Roman arena and other ruins) and **Narbonne**.

One of the region's most potentially important attractions, its Mediterranean coastline, has until recently remained undeveloped.

Carcassonne: ancient fortifications (Photo Commissariat Général au Tourisme)

This has been largely because much of the area was infested with mosquitoes, as well as the fact that transport and services were inadequate.

New Resorts However, a vast project by the French government has succeeded in overcoming these problems. The mosquitoes have been virtually eliminated, roads have been built and new Riviera-like resorts have been created at places like **La Grande-Motte** and **Canet-Plage**, which can cope with larger numbers of tourists than can be accommodated in the smaller traditional resorts such as **Collioure** and **Banyuls-sur-Mer**. Nine new yachting marinas have been built, providing facilities for 4500 yachts, and within six years of starting the scheme the number of visitors to the coastal resorts alone increased from 660 000 to over one and a quarter million. This part of the coast, with 200 km of sandy beaches, and known as the **Côte Vermeille** (the vermilion coast), is being developed into a major centre of tourism.

The Massif Central: Limousin and Auvergne

The **Massif Central** is the huge highland area which dominates much of the southern half of France. It has been called 'the roof of France'; just as with a roof, the rain runs off, not into the gutters but into the many rivers which rise in this area. These rivers are vital to the life of Central France, to provide water both for irrigation and water highways for the cheap transport of goods and produce.

It is an unspoiled area, formed by extinct volcanoes, with lakes, rivers, pine forests and pasture land.

Depopulation

The area has suffered from losing too many of its people to Paris and other towns, but is now benefiting from the expansion programmes which are intended to create new jobs and to develop the resources of the area.

The region is made up of the two ancient provinces of the **Limousin** and the **Auvergne**. Much of the life of the region is centred on the River Rhône and its major tributary, the Saône.

Limousin

The Limousin lies to the north-west of the region, and is an area of moorland and sheep, and in the valleys and lowlands cattle are reared.

Limoges is the ancient capital of the Limousin, as well as its largest town. It produces world-famous porcelain and enamel. In **Aubusson**

tapestries have been made for over 1200 years. It was here that the great tapestry in Coventry Cathedral was made.

Aubusson tapestries
(Photo P. J. Downes)

Auvergne

This is a beautiful area of rolling hills and lakes, and ancient villages with old houses and churches. Although many of the villages here have lost a lot of their inhabitants to the towns, tourists are attracted to the many spa-towns, including **Vichy**, famous not only for its spa-water, but as the war-time capital of unoccupied France under its notorious leader Laval. The capital and largest industrial town in the Auvergne is **Clermont-Ferrand**, with a population of over 200 000 people.

Les Causses

This is to the south of the Auvergne and is an area of bare plateaux, caves, and underground rivers, with few inhabitants other than the sheep, whose milk is used to produce the famous *Roquefort* cheese.

Industry

Nearly a quarter of France's coal is produced in the region, based on **Saint-Etienne** and **Le Creusot**, which also produce iron and steel.
The other main industries are textiles, and motor tyres: three-quarters of France's tyres are produced in the area, by the Michelin works at **Clermont-Ferrand** and Dunlop's at **Montluçon**.

The Rhône/Saône Valley

This is a valley formed by the Rhône and its great tributary the Saône, which flows down from eastern France near the Rhine. The combined river system forms the main axis of southern France and is a waterway linking the Mediterranean and southern France with central France, and by means of the canal system, with the Rhine and the waterways of Germany.

Agriculture

The wines produced in this area are amongst the most famous in France and include *Beaujolais* and *Burgundy, Mâcon* and *Côtes du Rhône* (from the Valence area).

The poorer soils of the area are devoted to forestry, with cattle and dairy farming (butter and cheese) in the areas of richer soils, as well as wheat, maize and tobacco, sugar beet and fruit (peaches, apricots, cherries, apples and pears).

The Valley of the Rhône and orchards to the south of Vienne. On the left is the eastern edge of the Massif Central, and in the foreground the village of Ampuis. Vienne is in the distance (Photo Alain Perceval – DF)

Mistral

An important aspect of the climate is the *Mistral*, a strong, cold wind, which blows down the Rhône Valley from the Massif Central. This seems to be blowing incessantly and is something that the inhabitants of the area are constantly aware of, and sometimes even afraid of. The Maritime Alps shelter the coastal strip of the Côte d'Azur from this wind. The *Mistral* has also given its name to the famous express train which runs from Paris to the south, and which is one of the prestigious trains of the French Railways.

Industry

Lyons, which lies at the point where the Saône joins the Rhône, is the largest city of the area (as well as the second city in France). It is the only city in the country, apart from Paris, with a population of over a million people.

Formerly the capital of Roman Gaul, Lyons has a medieval university, and still continues its traditional trade of manufacturing silk, of which it is the main centre in France. It is one of the largest producers of man-made textiles, and has a wide variety of industries, including electrical equipment, vehicles (buses and heavy lorries), chemicals and leather goods.

Expansion As well as being a major route centre for road, rail and water transport, Lyons is a town in the process of considerable expansion. Its growth is based on power supplied by coal from the nearby mining and industrial towns of **Saint-Etienne**, and by the hydro-electric power generated in the Alps.

The Rhône Valley

The valley of the Rhône stretches from Lyons to the Mediterranean, near Marseilles. Since 1934 it has been the subject of an ambitious plan to develop the Rhône in order to produce a major waterway, a major source of electrical power, and a system of irrigation to allow the development of the surrounding countryside. Great new hydro-electric works are being constructed and these will generate the electricity necessary for the creation of new industries.

Marseilles-Fos Metropolitan Area

Marseilles, with a population of just under a million, is France's busiest sea port, and its third largest town (after Paris and Lyons). Its port was first created by the Greeks, about 600 years before Christ; but after a period of decline, the port has been greatly expanded during the last 100 years to cater for the oil trade and the trade with North Africa (and France's former colonies).

Modern development of the Rhône
valley (Photo Brigaud – EDF)

Marseilles: the old port and the
modern motorway interchange
(Photo Jahan – DF)

Harbour As Marseilles could not expand any further because of its position at the foot of the mountains, the port of Marseilles has been extended into the Gulf of Fos. The combined area makes an enormous harbour complex, with 25 km of wharves, piers and other harbour installations, and handles nearly 40 per cent of France's sea trade.

Oil Altogether the Marseilles-Fos Metropolitan Area covers 2800 square km and its industries are expanding rapidly, not just in the port area. To cope with the oil trade, massive oil storage tanks, oil refineries and petro-chemical installations have been constructed, and these stand out among all the factories for the engineering, electronic, aeronautical, chemical and food industries.

Agriculture

The hot sunny climate, which has now been combined with the benefits of irrigation from the rivers, provides good conditions for agriculture. In spite of an increasing amount of land being taken up for other uses such as industry and housing etc., wine, wheat, rice, fruit, vegetables and flowers are grown, and sheep, pigs and poultry are reared.

Fishing

Marseilles is France's main 'sardine port', with catches of over 5000 tonnes a year.

Provence and the Côte d'Azur (Riviera) and Corsica

Provence covers a part of the Mediterranean area as well as a large area inland which is often known as the **Midi**, and is one of the most beautiful areas in Europe. It is a region of hot sun and magnificent scenery, which is shown to its best advantage by the brilliant clear light of the area, which has long attracted scores of painters. The coastal region, in the south-east corner, known as the **Côte d'Azur** or the **Riviera**, is one of the most famous tourist playgrounds in Europe, and adjoins the Italian border and the principality of Monaco (with its capital of Monte-Carlo) to the east.

Provence

Provence is mainly a hilly, inland region, with areas of pine forest and grazing for sheep. There are many spectacular gorges, and wheat, maize and vegetables are grown on the slopes; all sorts of fruit,

Aix-en-Provence: the elegant avenue of the Cours Mirabeau in the town centre (Photo Ceta-Aix)

including oranges, lemons, vines, figs and olives are grown in the valleys. In the mountains bauxite is mined to produce aluminium (of which it is the raw material) for the aerospace industry at **Toulouse** as well as for many other industrial uses.

Roman influence As the name implies, this was an important 'Province' of Roman Gaul, and there are many Roman (and Greek) remains, including the magnificent amphitheatres at **Orange**, **Nîmes** and **Arles** (which seats 25 000 spectators) and other remains at **Avignon** (famous for its bridge and Pope's Palace). Also at Nîmes is the superb Roman aqueduct, the **Pont du Gard**. Constructed in 19 BC it has three storeys, and is a remarkable piece of engineering for its time.

The ancient capital of Provence is the university town of **Aix-en-Provence**, which holds an important annual festival of the arts.

Climate

The special nature of its climate results from the fact that it not only enjoys long periods of hot Mediterranean sunshine, but is sheltered from the rains and winds (including the *Mistral*) by the Maritime Alps, which act as a kind of barrier running along the coast just inland. The effect of these mountains is that the Riviera has all the advantages of water from the mountains, but without the rain! Hence it has what many people consider to be an ideal climate: mild winters, and long, hot, dry summers, with little or no rain often for months on end.

Agriculture and industry

The climate, which is ideal for holidays, makes the area ideal for growing fruit and vegetables, and in particular flowers, many of which go to the perfume factories of **Grasse**, just inland from Cannes.

Tourism and the Côte d'Azur (Riviera)

The Riviera was originally 'discovered' in the nineteenth century by the English (led by Lord Brougham, whose statue stands in the middle of Cannes), as a place for winter holidays, because of its mild winters. The explosion of the summer tourist trade has taken place only since the end of World War II, and the Riviera has now been extended from the Italian border in the east as far west as Marseilles.

The combination of hot sun and warm sea now brings hordes of tourists from all over Europe, and has resulted in almost every town and village along the coast being largely devoted to tourism. The many camp-sites bring additional holiday-makers, and overcrowding is now a real problem. Many of the resorts are among the most famous in the world: **Nice**, **Cannes**, **Juan-Les-Pins**, **Saint-Raphaël**, **Saint-Tropez**. The two largest of these are the elegant Cannes, with its harbour and luxury yachts, and the larger and more bustling Nice (population nearly 400 000). The famous Battle of Flowers is held here in Lent, when brightly-decorated floats are driven in a procession, and their occupants pelt each other (and spectators) with flowers. During the long summer season the beaches of these and many other smaller resorts are packed with holidaymakers soaking up the sun and bathing in the sea. Apart from the attractions of the beach, these resorts have a variety of hotels, restaurants and entertainments. The relative cool of the evening is the time when people enjoy the delights of French cooking, often eating outside on the *terrasses* of the restaurants, or stroll along the colourful streets until the small hours of the morning.

Corsica

Corsica is a Mediterranean island about 178 km from the French coast, with a population of about 300 000. Until 1763 it was Italian, and even today the dialect sounds like a form of Italian.

The climate and scenery are quite similar to those of the Côte d'Azur, though until recently Corsica has had a reputation as a wild and untamed island, famous for its brigands and vendettas, and as the birthplace of Napoleon, who was born in the capital, Ajaccio. Nowadays, there is a developing tourist industry which is bringing new wealth and new ways of life to the island. This is part of the French government's plan to develop the regions, and in this case to take advantage of Corsica's natural assets: the attractions to tourists of its climate and position. The plans include schemes to improve transport, provide new hotels (with an extra quarter of a million beds) and build yachting marinas. The result is that Corsica is increasingly taking part in the 'boom industry' of Mediterranean tourism.

The yachting harbour at Menton
(Photo P. B. Houldsworth)

Corsica (Photo Commissariat Général de Tourisme*)*

The French Alps: Savoy-Dauphiny

Some of the most spectacular scenery in Europe is to be found in the French Alps, which include the highest peak in Europe: **Mont Blanc** at 4800 m. It is a region of snow-capped peaks, gorges, forests, lakes and pastures and its variety and beauty attract tourists from all over the world. Many of the peaks are covered in snow all the year round, and this is perhaps the best-known winter-sports area in the world, centred not only on such famous resorts as **Chamonix**, but also on a host of new resorts which have mushroomed up all over the area to take advantage of the winter-sports boom. As well as the resorts for winter-sports, summer lake-resorts such as **Aix-Les-Bains** and **Annecy** attract many thousands of summer visitors.

Farming

In spite of the mountainous nature of the countryside, various types of farming are carried on. The traditional kind of farming is cattle-rearing. The animals graze on the lower slopes in early summer and then go up to the higher slopes for two or three months in mid-summer. Dairy products, such as butter and cheese are produced; in particular the local cheese, *Gruyère*.

The lush, green valleys favour the cultivation of wheat, oats, maize and orchards of plums, apples and cherries.

Industry

The main centre of industry is the dynamic and expanding town of **Grenoble**, which shares silk and rayon-production with Lyons, and specialises in the manufacture of gloves and leather goods.

As well as being a university town, Grenoble is the intellectual, administrative and cultural capital of the Alpine area. Its attractions have made it the most rapidly expanding city in France, and for many people a genuine counter-attraction to Paris; so much so that in recent years it has been something of a French 'boom town'. The population more than doubled in 30 years: it increased from 80 000 in 1945 to 170 000 in 1975.

Grenoble (Photo P. J. Downes)

SECTION E: FRANCE'S PAST

KINGS AND RULERS OF FRANCE

Romans	59 B.C. – 395 A.D.	Roman Occupation of Gaul
Early Kings	481 – 751	The Merovingians
	751 – 987	The Carolingians (including Charlemagne: 768 – 814)
	987 – 1328	Capetians (founded by Hugh Capet: 987 – 996)
	1329 – 1589	Valois (including François I: 1515 – 1547)
Bourbon Kings	1589 – 1792	1589 – 1610: Henri IV 1610 – 1643: Louis XIII 1643 – 1715: Louis XIV (*Le Roi Soleil*) 1715 – 1774: Louis XV 1774 – 1792: Louis XVI
Revolution 1789	1792 – 1799	The Republic
	1799 – 1804	The Consulate
	1804 – 1815	Napoleon and the First Empire
Restoration	1815 – 1824	Louis XVIII
	1824 – 1830	Charles X
	1830 – 1848	Louis–Philippe I
	1848 – 1852	The Second Republic
	1852 – 1870	Napoleon III and the Second Empire
Republics	1870 – 1939	Third Republic
	1940 – 1944	German Occupation
	1945 – 1958	Fourth Republic
	1958 – 1969	Fifth Republic, and de Gaulle
	1969 – 1974	President Pompidou
	1974 – 1981	President Giscard d'Estaing
	1981 –	President Mitterrand

Origins and early history

Prehistoric Era (18 000–20 000 BC)

The earliest people to live in what is now known as France lived about 20 000 years ago in the south-west of France in the Périgord. It is in this area at Lascaux that evidence of their life and the animals they hunted has been found. In 1940 caves were discovered in which the walls were covered with coloured paintings of horses, bison, mammoths, rhinoceros, etc. These paintings are quite outstanding in quality and realism.

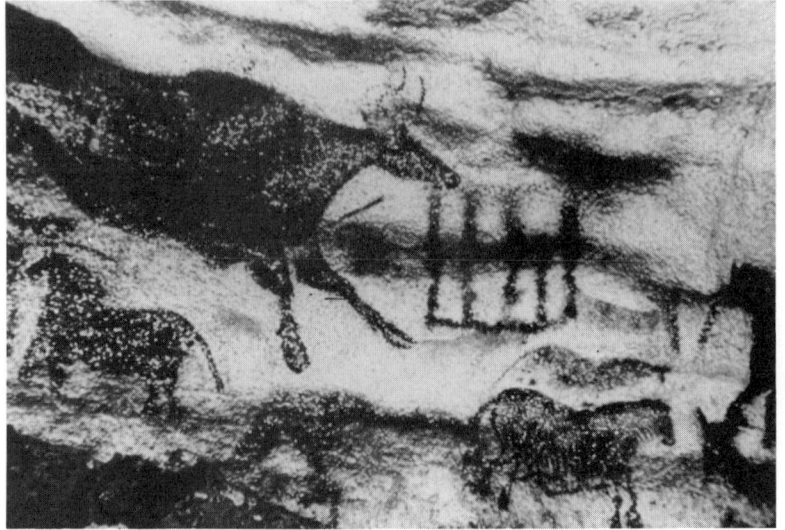

The prehistoric wall paintings in the caves at Lascaux

Bronze Age (2000 BC)

Traces of other early peoples have been found in the north-west in Brittany. Lines and circles of stones, called *menhirs*, still stand today, rather like Stonehenge in Britain. They are thought to have been part of some religious ceremonies performed by a people who lived about

The ancient stone monuments or menhirs (Photo P. J. Downes)

4000 years ago. These people brought with them agriculture, cattle and primitive metal industries.

The Gauls (1000 BC)

About 3000 years ago the war-like Celts carried out a series of invasions. Those Celts who settled in what is now France were called Gauls. They were able to turn their skill and energy, which had been so effective in war, to clearing forests, cultivating the land, and making some of the early roads. These were the people whom the Romans had to conquer 1000 years later.

Roman Gaul (59 BC–395 AD)

In 59 BC the Roman armies under Julius Caesar invaded Celtic Gaul, and in a period of about eight years they had overcome the resistance of the Gauls and their leader, Vercingetorix.

The period of the Roman occupation of Gaul is the setting for the popular series of stories and pictures based on the Adventures of Astérix, who was supposedly a Gaul who lived under the Roman occupation.

The period of Roman rule lasted between four and five centuries, during which Gaul became a province of the Roman Empire, at that time the most powerful in the world. The Romans brought with them not only their military power but also their civilisation, the benefits of which are still felt today.

This was a very important period in the development of the country that was later to become France. The Romans left behind many traces

Astérix the Gaul

Nîmes (Languedoc): the Roman arena, built to hold 20 000 spectators (Nîmes was founded at the beginning of the first century by Emperor Augustus.) (Photo Alain Perceval – DF)

which are still visible: the road system in France today is still based on the Roman road system, and the French legal system is based on Roman Law. The Romans were also great builders, not merely of roads, but of towns and buildings. A number of France's most beautiful towns owe much of their character to the Romans, who built amphitheatres, temples, arenas, etc., many of which still remain for us to admire: Arles, Nîmes, Narbonne, Vienne and Lyons, which was the early capital of the Roman Province, (hence the name 'Provence'), were all prosperous centres of Roman civilisation. Eventually their influence spread throughout France, and included *Lutetia*, the Roman name for Paris, which became the capital of all Roman Gaul. Roman influence and prosperity lasted for over four centuries, until the fall of Rome in 395 AD.

Fifth century AD: barbarian invasions

After the fall of the Roman Empire, Gaul no longer had the Roman armies to protect it. In the century following the withdrawal of the Romans, Gaul was exposed to the invasions of a number of barbarian tribes from the east, i.e., what is now largely Germany and Scandinavia. One of the most important of these tribes was the Franks.

Clovis and the Franks (the Merovingian kings)

The Franks, who originally came from Germany, gave their name to the country which was eventually to become France. Their great king was Clovis, who led the conquest of Gaul, which began in 486 AD, and whose conversion to Christianity and subsequent baptism at Reims in 496 was an important influence in the spread of Christianity throughout the country.

Charlemagne and the Carolingian Empire

In the year 771 the great Charlemagne became king of the Franks and the whole of their empire, which included France, Germany and Italy and a large part of western Europe. It was Charlemagne (meaning Charles the Great) who laid the foundations of modern Europe, with one church, one language, one civilisation and one king, Charlemagne, at the centre of it all, ruler of Church and state. He was in effect emperor of Europe, with his seat at Aix-la-Chapelle. He was famous not only as a leader in battle but for his peace-time achievements: the effective organisation of his huge empire, his system of justice, and his encouragement of scholars and education. So we see that thanks to Charlemagne there was already a United Europe over a thousand years ago!

From the Middle Ages to the Renaissance

The Capetian kings (987–1328)

With the invasions of the Norsemen came the feudal period, when the power of the kings was weakened and replaced by the power of the feudal lords and barons; living in their great castles, they maintained their own armies of vassals who had to work and fight for them.

This is the period in which many of the great medieval buildings we see today were built: the great fortresses or castles, the Gothic cathedrals and monastries, which were a magnificent expression not only of architecture, but of sculpture, painting and stained glass. A new enthusiasm was discovered for learning, and universities were founded at Paris, Toulouse and Montpellier. It was also a period of more refined manners, which found their expression in the chivalry of the baronial courts, where the *troubadours* (or travelling poets and singers) entertained the knights and their ladies with their poems, which they recited or sang, often accompanying themselves on the lute (rather like the modern guitar).

The Conciergerie: the medieval fortress-prison in the centre of Paris (Photo P. J. Downes)

The Valois kings (1328–1589)

Hundred Years War The first half of this period was dominated by the Hundred Years War (1337–1453) between France and England. During this war the English invaded and occupied most of western France, and fought many famous battles, including those at Crécy, Calais, Poitiers and Agincourt, which were great English victories.

Joan of Arc

Joan of Arc: a statue standing in Orleans, where she led the French into battle against the English armies in 1429 (Photo P. J. Downes)

The French later gained inspiration from the leadership of Joan of Arc, a young peasant girl later known as the Maid of Orleans, who led the French in breaking the siege of Orleans. She believed she was inspired by God to help France, but was later betrayed to the English armies who put her on trial for heresy and witchcraft. On conviction she was burnt at the stake at Rouen in 1431, though she was later made a saint.

The sixteenth century: François I (1515–1547) and the Renaissance

Renaissance – new learning The second half of the period was dominated by the movement known as the *Renaissance* (meaning Rebirth), which was a rediscovery or rebirth of learning during the sixteenth century in Europe. This rediscovery of ancient learning was reflected in the work of French writers, artists, and architects, who were inspired by the classical Greeks and Romans. This was the period

The meeting between François I (on right) and Henry VIII of England on the Field of the Cloth of Gold (*Photo* Musées Nationaux)

when so many of the *châteaux*, both in the Loire Valley and in the Ile de France, were built. Writers such as Rabelais and Montaigne expressed the new joy of learning.

François I The Renaissance was at its height during the reign of the great king, François I, who encouraged the new tastes for luxury, art and learning. It was François who invited architects from Italy, which was the seat of the Renaissance, to build the palaces of Chambord and Fontainebleau, and large parts of the Louvre and the Tuileries in Paris. Among the great artists and scholars who were attracted from Italy by François was perhaps the greatest figure of them all, Leonardo da Vinci, who was installed by François in a beautiful *château* outside Amboise. The interior of this has been recently restored and filled with furniture of the period, as well as a number of models of his inventions and reproductions of his drawings.

Louis XIV and the classical period

Le Grand Siècle (seventeenth century)

The seventeenth century was almost certainly the greatest period in the history of France. During this period France was the greatest power in Europe, which in effect meant the greatest power in the world. She was also the richest country in Europe, had Europe's most powerful army and was the cultural centre of Europe.

Louis XIV (1643–1715) – 'The Sun King'

When Louis XIV came to the throne in 1643, he carried on the development of France which had taken place under Louis XIII, his father, and before him, under François I.

Louis gathered together a brilliant team of advisers and civil servants to help him achieve his ambition, which was to be the absolute monarch and master of France. He was known as *Le Roi-Soleil*, ('The Sun King'): he was the sun from which France derived all her light, and the centre of the universe as far as France was concerned. He claimed that he was the state: *'L'état, c'est moi.'*

Versailles: an aerial view showing the enormous château *and the formal gardens and fountains*

Louis XIV – portrait painted by Rigaud in 1701

Molière, whose great comedies were performed for the king and the Court (Photo DF)

Versailles and the court

In order to show his greatness to France and the world, as well as to house his enormous court, he built a large and magnificent palace at Versailles, outside Paris. This was a personal triumph for him in every sense:

It is an outstanding piece of classical architecture and planning.

It took nearly 50 years to complete and required an army of 36 000 workmen.

Politically it made it possible for him to control the nobles, bringing them all together under one roof where he could keep an eye on them and dominate them. Over 1000 courtiers were housed in the palace (with 4000 servants to wait on them). Louis' own staff amounted to 10 000 people.

Culturally, it provided the scene for bringing together many of the most brilliant men of the period: dramatists such as Corneille, Racine and Molière; philosophers such as Pascal and Descartes; painters such as Poussin, and musicians such as Lully and Couperin. These men ensured that this was the great period (or *grande époque*) for France in a cultural sense as well as in every other sense.

The eighteenth century

After reaching the peak of her greatness in the seventeenth century under Louis XIV, France gradually lost much of her power during the eighteenth century, under Louis XV and Louis XVI. Yet the cultural influence of France, and of Paris in particular, remained as great as ever.

Thinkers

It was a period of great thinkers and philosophers such as Jean-Jacques Rousseau, Voltaire and Montesquieu, who criticised the state of affairs in France – the existing institutions, the idea that kings had a divine right to rule and the lack of freedom of thought and religion.

Unrest in France

France was no longer a powerful military country: her finances had been weakened by wars (she had lost the Seven Years War) and by the extravagance of the Court. By contrast the people, particularly the peasantry, were poor, and often had not enough to eat. Their situation was made even worse by the heavy taxes they had to pay in order to support the Court; and they were thrown into prison if they could not pay. All these factors combined to create a deep sense of unrest and discontent in the country.

The French Revolution and Napoleon Bonaparte

14 July 1789: storming of the Bastille

The situation blew up in 1789, when on 14 July the Bastille, which was the main fortress and prison of Paris (rather like the Tower of London) was attacked and the prisoners freed. Many of the nobles fled from their estates, and terrible massacres took place. This storming of the Bastille was the spark which set off the French Revolution, one of the great turning-points not only in French history but in European history. The 14 July has ever since been celebrated as a national *fête*. A National Assembly was set up, which adopted a constitution based on the 'Declaration of the Rights of Man'.

Effects of the Revolution

Absolute monarchy was overthrown and the power given to the people. The nobles lost their privileges.

'The Declaration of the Rights of Man' proclaimed the principles of the revolution based on 'Liberty, Equality and Fraternity'; that the aim of society is the common good; and that all men are equal before the law.

The old provinces were replaced by the *départements*, which still exist today.

The storming of the Bastille, 1789 (Photo Musées Nationaux)

1792: The First Republic

In 1792 the king was dethroned by the National Convention, which proclaimed the Republic, and for a time the Assembly was controlled by extremists.

Reign of terror

A reign of terror was launched, led by extremist revolutionary leaders such as Robespierre, Danton and Marat. The king, Louis XVI, was executed, and with him not only nobles, but also many people of moderate views went to the guillotine. Among those who were executed were the Queen (Marie-Antoinette), the poet André Chenier, and the chemist Lavoisier (who discovered so much about oxygen). Guillotines were set up in a number of public squares in Paris, including the Place de la Concorde, which was formerly known as the Place de la Révolution, as a reminder of what happened there during the revolution.

Napoleon Bonaparte – a propaganda picture of the time. Napoleon is shown as First Consul, replacing his sword after the Declaration of Peace (Photo BN – Paris)

Napoleon Bonaparte

After the revolution, France was involved in a number of foreign wars, conducted with the aim of spreading the revolution throughout Europe. One of the generals who emerged from these campaigns was Napoleon Bonaparte, a Corsican who had trained to become a soldier at French military schools. He proved himself to be a brilliant military leader and was already a general by the age of 26.

In 1799 he became one of the three consuls to rule France.

In 1804 he became emperor, and crowned himself in the cathedral of Notre-Dame in Paris.

During the period of the Empire, Napoleon introduced a number of reforms, and even today France enjoys the benefits of many of these.

Napoleon's reforms

Law: The *Code Napoléon* is not only the basis of modern French law, but this in turn is the basis of Common Market law, which has to be followed by all member countries.

Education: A new system of secondary education, based on the *lycées*, or grammar schools, was set up. These have for many years been one of the pillars of French education, and still exist today, though modified by recent reorganisation.

Administration: A system of prefects, who were responsible for the administration of departments, was introduced, and still operates in many similar ways today.

Banking: The Bank of France was established, and is still very much alive.

Honours: The Legion of Honour was introduced, and is still one of France's greatest honours.

Napoleon at the Battle of Wagram

Napoleonic Wars

Napoleon unfortunately did not confine his activities to reforms. He undertook a number of wars with the aim of conquering Europe and setting himself up as its dictator. To begin with he had some important victories, e.g. Austerlitz, Jena, Eylau and Wagram. (These are commemorated in Paris on the Arc de Triomphe.) It was a period of great splendour for Napoleon and the French army, who between them succeeded in conquering most of western Europe.

In 1812, Napoleon made the mistake of trying to conquer Russia. With his *grande armée* of 650 000 men he invaded Russia, and succeeded in entering Moscow, but he found that the Russians had retreated, setting fire to the empty capital. By this time the Russian winter was setting in and the French army had no food; so Napoleon was forced to retreat, and during his retreat from Moscow most of his army froze to death. Of the 650 000 who set out, only 50 000 came back. This was the beginning of the end for Napoleon.

European Alliance

Virtually the whole of Europe rose against Napoleon, and over a million men were mustered by the Alliance (a combination of European states), which defeated the French army at the Battle of Leipzig in 1813.

Abdication and exile

Napoleon was forced to abdicate and was exiled to the island of Elba in the Mediterranean.

1815: Escape and the 'Hundred Days' War'

In 1814, the Allies met at a Congress in Vienna to try to resolve the problems of Europe. While they were still meeting, Napoleon escaped from Elba and landed in the south of France. He immediately set out to rally his armies and marched on Paris. However, Europe united once more and in 1815, after a campaign lasting a hundred days, Napoleon was defeated again at Waterloo by the combined armies of the British, under the Duke of Wellington, and the Prussians under Blücher.

Napoleon was imprisoned on the Atlantic island of St Helena, where he remained for six years until he died in 1821.

The nineteenth century

The Restoration: Louis XVIII and Charles X

Louis-Philippe (Photo Archives Documentation Française)

After Napoleon's defeat and exile to St Helena, the monarchy was restored under Louis XVIII (who was the brother of Louis XVI) from 1815–24; and then by Charles X (1825–30), who tried to put the clock back to the *Ancien Régime*, the time before the revolution.

1830 Revolution and Louis-Philippe (1830–1848)

In the Revolution of 1830 Charles was forced to abdicate. He was replaced by Louis-Philippe, who was supported by the *bourgeoisie*, the professional middle class, which had taken over from the nobility after the 1789 revolution as the dominant element in France. Under Louis-Philippe a more liberal system was introduced, and parliamentary government was established.

1848 Revolution

It was also a period of growing unrest among the workers whose demands for social reform were being voiced more and more strongly.

Although nearly ten million people paid taxes, less than a quarter of a million were allowed to vote and this was another important cause of unrest. It was the demand for social reform that led to the revolution of 1848 and the fall of Louis-Philippe.

Delacroix

The arts During this period France reasserted her cultural greatness through the works of novelists such as Balzac, Stendhal and Flaubert, Romantic poets such as Vigny and Hugo, musicians such as Hector Berlioz, and painters such as Ingres and Delacroix.

Louis-Napoleon: President of the Republic (1849–1852)

1849 The vote As a result of the revolution of 1848, a republic was set up: universal suffrage, with its principle of 'one man, one vote,' was established. This republic elected as its president Louis-Napoleon, the nephew of Napoleon Bonaparte, and was known as the 'bourgeois republic'.

1852–1870: Emperor Napoleon III and the Second Empire

In 1852 Louis-Napoleon had himself crowned Emperor Napoleon III. This was the beginning of the Second Empire, which covered the period of the third quarter of the century.

It was a period of commercial and industrial prosperity in France, and produced many improvements and new buildings; new boulevards (inspired by Baron Haussmann) were built in Paris. During this period the industrial revolution began to get underway.

1870: The Franco-Prussian War

This was the first of several conflicts between France and Prussia, the most powerful state of what is now Germany. Among the many causes of this war were Napoleon's need to restore his popularity in France, and the need of Prussia's leader, Bismarck, to defeat France so that she could not prevent him from forming a united Germany.

In this war, Napoleon himself was captured, and from September 1870 to January 1871 Paris was besieged by the Prussian army. Conditions were so bad during the siege that the people, close to starvation, were reduced to eating dogs and rats. At the end of January, Paris fell and the king of Prussia was proclaimed emperor of Germany at Versailles.

Meanwhile, revolution had broken out in Paris, and in March 1871 the government of the Commune, elected by the workers of Paris, was set up.

1870–1940: The Third Republic

The Third Republic was born out of the French defeat in the Franco-Prussian War (in which France lost Alsace and part of Lorraine to Germany). This republic, with a president at its head, began with a period of peace and prosperity lasting forty years.

Prosperity

The Industrial Revolution, which had begun in the 1850s and 1860s during the Second Empire, was creating new wealth and prosperity. For this reason the period has often been called *La Belle Epoque*, rather in the sense of 'The Good Old Days'. Certain social reforms were introduced, including income tax and compulsory free education, but it was also a time of social conflict, with the rise of trade unions and socialist ideas.

Growth of towns More and more people were leaving agriculture and their homes in the country because they were attracted to the money and jobs in the towns. This movement of people away from the country, which has been called the 'rural exodus', was a process which was to continue until after World War II.

Colonisation

Overseas, this period saw the growth of the French colonies: Morocco, Tunisia, the Congo, Nigeria, Indo-China and Madagascar all became French possessions. As a result, France became the second largest colonial power in the world, after Great Britain.

The arts

In the arts, France continued during this period to produce important figures: novelists like Emile Zola, Anatole France and Paul Bourget; the great short-story writer Guy de Maupassant; poets like Verlaine and Rimbaud; philosophers such as Henri Bergson; and composers like Bizet and Debussy. This was in particular the great period of French painting, and produced a number of important painters: Monet, Degas,

The composer Debussy

Pierre and Marie Curie at work in their laboratory, where they discovered the radio-active element radium

Cézanne, Renoir, Gauguin. Van Gogh, although he was born in Holland, is considered to be largely French, as much of his best work was done whilst he was living in France.

Science

This was also a period of great scientific discovery in France. Louis Pasteur is famous for his research into infections and the nature of bacilli. The word 'pasteurise', which we use to refer to the process of sterilising milk, comes directly from his name. Pierre and Marie Curie were a brilliant team of husband and wife who in 1895 discovered radio-activity and the new element radium. In 1909 Louis Blériot ensured himself a place in history as one of the great pioneers of aviation by becoming the first man to fly the channel. This was a tremendous news story, and early news reels still exist of Blériot and the flimsy-looking aeroplane he used for his historic flight.

Louis Blériot and the early monoplane in which he made his historic first crossing of the Channel by air (Photo Archives Documentation Française)

The twentieth century

World War I (1914–1918) and its consequences

This was on a far larger scale than the war of 1870, and was one of the most terrible wars in history. Though it involved Germany invading France for the second time, it was not limited like the 1870 war to just France and Germany: most of Europe and a large part of the rest of the world, including the USA and Canada, Australia, New Zealand and Japan were also drawn into it.

A number of terrible battles were fought, such as those of the Somme, the Marne, Ypres, Verdun, in which thousands and even hundreds of thousands of men were killed in a single battle. The cemeteries where many of these men are buried are still neatly maintained, with rows and rows of military graves often stretching as far as the eye can see.

Effects of the war

Although the war ended with France on the winning side, the country was exhausted. Over one and a quarter million French soldiers, the men on whom France's future would have been built, were dead, and there were hardly any families in France who had not lost somebody in the war.

A large area of northern France, which was the scene of so many battles, was devastated: factories, farms and communications were destroyed. Even today the effects can be seen in many towns and cities of northern France, where much of the building dates from after 1918.

Above, the exterior and below the interior of the Maginot Line (Photos Documentation Française Photothèque)

The period between the wars: 1919–1939

This period was characterised by France's efforts to recover from the war which was finally ended by the Treaty of Versailles in 1919. In 1933 Hitler came to power in Germany and rapidly expanded the country's armed forces, posing a considerable threat to peace in Europe. During the period before the war France constructed a line of defensive posts along the German frontier, known as the 'Maginot Line'.

Yet none of the measures taken by France was very successful, for when war came in 1939 France, like many other countries, was not properly prepared, and neither her army nor her economy had been brought up to date. Her industries and even her birth rate were actually in decline.

France and World War II (1939–1945)

The war began with Germany's invasion of Poland in 1939. Between then and 1940 was the period of the so-called 'phoney war', when there were no major battles, but merely skirmishes between the Maginot Line and its German equivalent, the Siegfried Line.

In 1940 history repeated itself when the Germans invaded Belgium, Holland and Luxembourg, as they had during World War I. The effect of this was to allow the German army to get round the back of the Maginot Line, without having to fight its way through it. France was invaded and Paris occupied.

The British army and part of the French army managed to embark at Dunkirk for England, thanks to a massive rescue operation in the English Channel, involving hundreds of small boats, yachts and even pleasure steamers (as well as British warships). Private yachtsmen and owners of small boats from all round Britain's coasts volunteered to help in the evacuation. This successful British rear-guard action enabled 350 000 men, who were surrounded by German troops, to make their way to Britain. (It is perhaps fair to point out that the Dunkirk action does not have the same heroic associations for many Frenchmen, for whom it represented the final episode in the fall of France.)

In June 1940 the French accepted defeat, and Marshall Pétain, a World War I general, signed an armistice. In a month of fighting 100 000 French soldiers had been killed.

A puppet government was set up by the Germans at Vichy, under Pierre Laval, who, to the disgust of many of his fellow Frenchmen, collaborated with the Germans.

The German Occupation: 1940–1945 This was one of the most unhappy periods in all of France's long history. The French army had been defeated and the nation had to suffer the agony and humiliation of occupation. For most French people there was the constant fear of arrest by the Gestapo and deportation either to concentration camps or to forced labour.

The Resistance Many French men and women actively resisted the Germans, and a secret Resistance movement was organised. Its activities included:

Sabotaging German communication lines.

Acting as a massive intelligence network to relay information to London.

Helping allied airmen shot down over France to escape back to Britain (over 5000 succeeded).

Resistance workers were ruthlessly hunted down by the Gestapo. Many of them including the head of the Resistance, Jean Moulin (whose wartime code name was 'Max') were tortured to death. His successor was Georges Bidault, who later became prime minister after the war. During the period of the Occupation 30 000 French people

A wall plaque commemorating a Frenchman who died near this spot during the German occupation (1940–45)

ICI EST TOMBÉ
EAN ALBERT VOUILLARD
MORT EN SERVICE COMMANDÉ
ABATTU PAR LA GESTAPO
LE 17 MAI 1944 A 20 HEURES

ARC EN CIEL

were shot, and over a quarter of a million deported, of whom 160 000 died in captivity.

The *Maquis* acted as guerrilla groups and actively resisted the Germans, with the aid of weapons parachuted by allied planes.

The Free French On the fall of France in 1940, many French soldiers escaped to Britain to form a small but significant Free French army. Their leader was General de Gaulle who acted as a rallying point, not only to the Free French in England, but to the Resistance in France. He made a very moving broadcast to France in which he said: 'France has lost a battle, but she has not lost the war.' The symbol of the Free French was the cross of Lorraine (Lorraine was the birth-place of Joan of Arc.)

June 1944: Allied invasion of France On 'D' Day, 6 June 1944, the Allies landed in Normandy, and after fierce fighting managed to penetrate the Atlantic Wall, which was a line of defences built by the Germans along the Atlantic and Channel Coasts. Thus began the Liberation of France and of Europe, culminating in the defeat of Germany and her surrender at the armistice signed at Reims in 1945.

General de Gaulle visiting a village in Normandy (Photo L'Embassade de France)

The Cross of Lorraine

The post-war period

The period since the end of the war in 1945 has been a period of French recovery, which has been so dramatic that it has been called 'the French miracle'. Virtually a new industrial revolution has taken place in France.

The recovery has been related to two of the weaknesses which characterised France during the 1930s:

1. The decline in industry has been halted; industry and the economy as a whole have been transformed. Partly due to the devastation of French industry during the war, the French have been able to make virtually a fresh start in organising their industries. This has been reflected in the creation of Regions, as new, stronger economic units than the old *départements*; and of the new urban centres (the *métropoles*) as centres of industrial expansion.

2. The decline in the birth rate between the wars had been a cause of worry to many French people, who saw the population of France falling behind that of its main industrial competitors, such as Germany, Britain and Italy. In 1800 France had the largest population in Europe, yet over 100 years later it was less than that of either Britain or Germany.

	FRANCE	BRITAIN	GERMANY
1800	28 million	16 millions	22 millions
1910	41 millions	45 millions	63 millions

After 1945 the French birth rate rose more quickly even than that of Britain and Germany (though the rate since 1968 has dropped). This gave rise to a new feeling of optimism in the country, which spread to many walks of life.

The boost to morale was very important after the depression of war-time defeat and occupation, which had shocked many French people out of their pre-war attitudes.

The Plan

Soon after the Liberation, the first of several Plans was introduced, under the auspices of Jean Monnet, to help the French economy and industry.

The Treaty of Rome and the Common Market

This government planning was successful and industry grew rapidly. Even more growth was achieved when France signed the Treaty of Rome in 1957, which was the beginning of the EEC (the European Economic Community) or Common Market. This was of tremendous benefit to France and the French economy during the next ten years.

General de Gaulle and the Fifth Republic

In 1958 the French people's new sense of confidence was given a further boost by the election to power of General Charles de Gaulle. De Gaulle brought a new sense of authority to French government, which both before and after the war had been weakened by frequent changes.

De Gaulle was particularly concerned with restoring a sense of pride to the French nation. He introduced a number of policies and measures designed to raise the prestige of France both at home and abroad: he strengthened the French armed forces; France developed a nuclear bomb (at tremendous cost); the expensive Concorde programme was begun and the liner *France* was built; the new Paris airport, which was to be named the 'Charles de Gaulle Airport', and the Mont Blanc tunnel in the Alps were constructed, and many of Paris's buildings were cleaned and restored to their original splendour.

However, de Gaulle's very strengths developed into weaknesses. The new authority which he had brought to French government was becoming too strong and inflexible, and even included censorship of press, radio and television.

And in the economic field the projects and policies which he had launched to increase the prestige of France were so costly that they became a serious drain on the resources of the country.

Above, Charles de Gaulle: President of the Republic 1958–69 (Photo Jean-Marie Marcel – DF)

Below, Paris: the events of May 1968. Students demonstrating through the streets of Paris (Photo CNDP)

May 1968 uprising

Commonly called *'les événements de mai'*, this was a revolt which began in May 1968 amongst students in Paris against the system of education and the system of government. The movement spread to pupils in the *lycées*, and throughout France. Workers went on strike (though not always for the same reasons as the students.)

There were riots and pitched battles in Paris between the students and the police, who used violent measures to quell the students.

Resignation of de Gaulle

Although he survived an election after the uprising, de Gaulle resigned in 1969. This brought to an end a period which was dominated by one man, de Gaulle, more than almost any other period had been since the fall of Napoleon.

Achievement Yet although there were some undesirable aspects to his period of government, it is only fair to say that during these years de Gaulle played a great part in restoring France's position in the world: he brought stable and strong government; he helped to restore the economy; he strengthened the armed forces; he launched a number of prestigious projects (some perhaps too costly for the French economy to bear), including an independent nuclear bomb programme; and by taking a lead in the development of the Common

Market he gave France a stronger voice in the affairs of Europe and the world. Above all, these achievements, as well as the power of de Gaulle's own personality, and evident love of his country, helped restore France's pride in herself.

New strength When de Gaulle came to power France had been weak, both politically and economically, but she emerged from the period of his leadership as one of the leading powers in Europe, politically stable and with a booming economy.

After de Gaulle

Georges Pompidou When de Gaulle was in power as president of the republic, he was supported by his own party, known as the *Gaullistes*. The leader of this party, and prime minister, Georges Pompidou, was elected in 1969 as president in succession to de Gaulle. Pompidou, who had been a successful banker before he became a politician, maintained the continuity of many of de Gaulle's more enlightened policies, but at the same time ensured the return to a more liberal and democratic form of government. He introduced a slightly greater degree of freedom to French radio and television, and increased the influence of parliament. But his home policy was in general more concerned with encouraging the economic growth of France rather than with social reforms. In foreign affairs Pompidou had a less aggressive approach to other countries, and he cut down on some of de Gaulle's more extravagant prestigious projects; it was largely thanks to Pompidou that France agreed to accept Britain as a member of the Common Market.

Georges Pompidou, greeting Giscard d'Estaing, with de Gaulle in the background (Photo Présidence de la République*)*

Valéry Giscard d'Estaing (Photo Ministère de l'Economie et des Finances*)*

Giscard d'Estaing

When Georges Pompidou died in 1974, he was succeeded by Valéry Giscard d'Estaing, who had been a brilliant minister of finance under both de Gaulle and Pompidou, and had done a great deal to contribute to the economic achievements during the period of their government.

Social reforms When he himself was elected president, he showed a much greater awareness of the need for social reform, and one of his first measures shortly after coming to power was to reduce the voting age from 21 to eighteen. In 1975 he began the reform of French radio and television, which had been started by Pompidou; he abolished the state-controlled body which had been responsible for the censorship under de Gaulle, and replaced it by seven separate companies, including television programme companies for each of the three television networks, as well as another which organises all the radio networks. What is even more important is that Giscard d'Estaing guaranteed the freedom of all the networks, even though they did remain under state control.

Economic policy President Giscard was unfortunate in that he inherited the effects of the world economic crisis and the world-wide inflation triggered off by the dramatic rise in the price of oil, which hit France particularly, as she has very little oil of her own. His economic policy, which was spearheaded by his prime minister, Raymond Barre (a former professor of economics), included austerity measures, such as control of wages, as well as an energetic encouragement of exports.

Defeat However, in spite of these economic measures, France suffered the effects of the world-wide recession in trade which followed the oil crisis, and this led to rising inflation and widespread unemployment. These factors, together with Giscard's rather auto-cratic manner and the bad publicity he received over alleged scandals, all helped to undermine his popularity. The result was his election defeat in May 1981, at the end of his first seven-year term of office.

François Mitterrand

François Mitterrand, the Socialist candidate and one of the most experienced politicians in the country, was elected president, with the support of the Communist Party, at his third attempt. He became the first Socialist president of the Fifth Republic.

In 1971, M. Mitterrand had formed the French Socialist Party, and begun to build it into a popular movement, which finally brought him to power ten years later. In 1974, as candidate of a united left, he was defeated in the election against Giscard d'Estaing, having previously lost to de Gaulle in 1965.

Among his policies were promises to cut unemployment and create new jobs, raise taxation for the wealthy, increase basic wages and allowances, and nationalise some of France's largest companies.

François Mitterrand (Photo Keystone)

Victory for the left In an overwhelming victory for the left, the Socialist Party won an absolute majority in the parliamentary elections, giving President Mitterrand complete freedom in putting through his programme. With more than 60 per cent of the total seats going to the Socialists, many former ministers and leaders of the outgoing government, as well as the Communist Party, were defeated. However, for the first time since 1947, Communist ministers were appointed to the Cabinet.

The arts in the twentieth century

Literature The twentieth century has seen no weakening in France's contribution to the world of the arts. Many famous writers have emerged: Paul Valéry, Guillaume Apollinaire; the novelists Marcel Proust, André Gide, François Mauriac; and dramatists such as Jean Giraudoux and Jean Anouilh, and Jean-Paul Sartre, who combined both theatre and philosophy.

Painting and music In painting France is maintaining her position through Matisse, Braque and the Spanish-born Pablo Picasso, who spent most of his life and did most of his work in France. Some of the most creative and imaginative buildings of the twentieth century have been designed by the architect, Le Corbusier, whilst in the field of music Ravel (famous for his 'Boléro'), Milhaud and Poulenc are among the great names of this century.

British Library Cataloguing in Publication Data

Houldsworth, Peter
All about France.
1. France
I. Title
944.083'8   DC17

ISBN 0 340 25595 1

First published 1982
Third impression 1984

Printed and bound in Hong Kong for
Hodder and Stoughton Educational,
a division of Hodder and Stoughton Ltd,
Mill Road, Dunton Green, Sevenoaks, Kent,
by Colorcraft Ltd.